Influential Environment and Resources Cases in China (2024)

The Supreme People's Court of the PRC
Editor

Influential Environment and Resources Cases in China (2024)

人民法院出版社
PEOPLE'S COURT PRESS

Springer

Editor
The Supreme People's Court of the PRC
Environment and Resources Division
Beijing, China

ISBN 978-981-96-9561-4 ISBN 978-981-96-9562-1 (eBook)
https://doi.org/10.1007/978-981-96-9562-1

Jointly published with People's Court Press
The print edition is not for sale in China (Mainland). Customers from China (Mainland) please order the print book from: People's Court Press.

This Springer imprint is published by the registered company Springer Nature Singapore Pte Ltd.
The registered company address is: 152 Beach Road, #21-01/04 Gateway East, Singapore 189721, Singapore

Contents

Chapter 1
Environmental Pollution Case Against Nanjing ** Dyeing Company, Wang *rong et al

Basic Facts

The waste acid liquid generated in the production process of Nanjing ** Dyeing Company (hereinafter referred to as "the dyeing company") is a type of hazardous waste and should be delivered to qualified enterprises for disposal according to relevant provisions of the state. In September 2010, the dyeing company appointed Wang * to coordinate the disposal of the waste acid—Wang * then reached a verbal agreement with Wang *rong, the legal representative of Nanjing** chemicals company (hereinafter referred to as "the chemicals company"), on disposal of the waste acid at the price of CNY 580 per ton. However, the company was only qualified for distribution of hazardous chemicals, rather than disposal. Thereafter, the waste acid liquid generated by the dyeing company was delivered to Wang *rong (the chemicals company) for disposal. Huang *jun, then director of the dyeing company's tank area, knowing that Wang *rong did not have the qualifications for disposal, was responsible for directly coordinating Wang *rong to transport the waste acid, while Wang * was responsible for the payment for the waste acid disposal fees. In September 2013, Wang *rong, knowing that Ding *dong (handled in a separate action) had no qualifications for disposal of waste acid, reached a verbal agreement with Ding *dong on disposal at the cost of CNY 150 per ton, and instructed Xu *mi to drive a tank car to transport waste acid from the dyeing company directly to a vessel parked by Ding *dong at the Yiling Wharf in Jiangdu. By May 2014, waste acid delivered to Ding *dong for disposal had totaled 2,828.02 tons. During the period, Ding *dong instructed Sun *shan, Qian *lin, and others for multiple times to drive the vessel at night, and discharged 2,698.1 tons of waste acid directly into the riverway of Taidong River and Xintongyang Canal. Between them, Sun *shan was involved in the discharge of 1728.82 tons, and Qian *lin 318.78 tons. Another 129.92 tons of waste acid that Ding *dong had failed to discharge was seized later. The Jiangsu Science and Technology Consulting Center and the Jiangsu Provincial Academy of

Influential Environment and Resources Cases in China (2024),
https://doi.org/10.1007/978-981-96-9562-1_1

Environmental Science held upon expert demonstration and analysis that the aforesaid waste acid liquid generated by the dyeing company was hazardous waste mainly composed of sulfuric acid with large quantities of organic matters. The relatively high concentration of the sulfuric acid was strongly corrosive, and extremely harmful to living bodies, water bodies, and the environment. The large amount of organic waste remaining in the waste acid would also cause long-term cumulative damage to the biological environment.

Judgment

In the trial of first instance, the Primary People's Court of Gaoyou City of Jiangsu Province held that defendant, the dyeing company, knowing that defendant Wang *rong's chemical company had no qualification for disposal of waste acid, delivered waste acid generated during the production process to Wang *rong for disposal, thus violated the environmental law and provisions of the state; defendant Wang *rong, knowing that Ding *dong had no qualification for disposal of waste acid, still transferred the waste acid of the dyeing company to Ding *dong for disposal; defendant Xu *mi, knowing that the items he transported was waste chemical liquid and that Ding *dong might not have the ability to dispose of waste acid, assisted Wang *rong in the transportation; and defendants Sun *shan and Qian *lin, knowing that it was waste chemical liquid, still secretly discharged it against the provisions of the state, and ultimately lead to serious environmental pollution. All of the above constituted the crime of environmental pollution and should be determined as joint crime. While for defendants Wang *and Huang *jun, the directly liable persons in charge of the dyeing company, who should have known that Wang *rong had no qualification for disposal of waste acid, but still arranged transaction within their respective duties, resulting in serious environmental pollution. They should be held criminally liable for the crime environmental pollution. To avoid the high disposal cost of hazardous waste, the dyeing company, knowingly entrusted other entities with no qualifications for disposal to handle the waste, ultimately lead to serious environmental pollution. In consideration of the dyeing company's circumstances of crime and capacity of fine-payment, the court of first instance sentenced the dyeing company to a fine of CNY 20 million and other defendants to imprisonment ranging from one to five years with penalties for the crime of environmental pollution. After the second instance hearing, the Yangzhou Intermediate People's Court of Jiangsu Province affirmed the original judgment.

Significance

This case is a criminal case of environmental pollution involving water body pollution due to illegal disposal of hazardous waste. The judgment of the case was a successful attempt of the court in appropriately determining the amount of fines to be imposed upon different parties under the principle of suiting punishment to crime. According to the provisions of the Criminal Law of China, the amount of fines shall be determined based on the circumstances of the crime. In terms of fines for an entity, considerations should include the nature of the crime, the amount of illegal gains, the losses caused and other factors. In this case, to avoid the high disposal cost of hazardous waste, the dyeing company, knowing that others had no qualification for disposal, still entrusted disposal, ultimately leading to serious consequence of environmental pollution. The huge amount of disposal expenses avoided should be determined as the gains obtained through the criminal act.

Concurrently, the acts also had caused inevitably considerable expenses for the clean-up of the environmental pollution. According to relevant judicial interpretations, public and private property losses should include property losses directly caused by environmental pollution, reduced value because of the environmental pollution, and the expenses needed for necessary measures to prevent pollution expansion and elimination.

Therefore, the amount of public and private property losses shall be used as an important parameter in determining the fines. The people's court, taking into full account the capacity of payment of the company, determined the amount of fines based on the illegal gains obtained and the public and private property losses.

The judgment of criminal punishment supported the restoration of the damaged environment, and also served as an effective deterrent to urge other companies to handle hazardous waste in accordance with the law.

Courts and Members of the Collegial Bench

Court of First Instance: In Gaoyou Primary People's Court, Jiangsu, before Wu Jiaming, Ji Xiaohong, Chen Zhaohui

Court of Second Instance: In Yangzhou Intermediate People's Court, Jiangsu, before Yin Xiaotao, Li Chunrong, Hao Jiajia

Chapter 2
Criminal Case with Add-On Civil Public Interest Litigation Against He *Qiang on Illegal Killing of Endangered Species and Hunting

Basic Facts

From November 2014 to January 2015, when collecting fishes in the Dongtinghu National Nature Reserve in Hunan Province, He *qiang and Zhong *jun came to an agreement on killing wild migratory birds by poisoning with fish farmers and their helpers including Fang *hua, Long *ru, Long *ming, Tu *bao, Yu *qiu, Zhang *hai, and Ren *ping. He *qiang provided pesticides for poisoning and was responsible for purchasing and selling of the killed birds. Afterward, He *qiang and other persons repeatedly killed wild migratory birds in the nature reserve by poisoning, and the killed birds were all purchased by He *qiang and sold to Wang Qianping under the agency of Li *. On January 18, 2015, 63 migratory birds in eight bags successively purchased by He *qiang and Zhong *jun from Fang *hua and Yu *qiu were seized by staff members of the nature reserve administration in the Haoba Wharf located in Junshan District, Yueyang City. It was identified that the aforesaid 63 migratory birds died of poisoning. In particular, 12 cygnets and five white spoonbills were wild animals under state protection (Category II); there were also gray herons, tadorna ferrugineas, eurasian wigeons, anas poecilorhynchas, and night herons, 46 in total, all protected wild animals with important social, economic, and scientific research values. It was verified that the total value of the 63 wild migratory birds seized was CNY44,617.

The People's Procuratorate of Yueyanglou District, Hunan Province instituted a public prosecution in the People's Court of Yueyanglou District, Yueyang City on the ground that He *qiang and other six persons committed a crime of illegal hunting and killing of rare and endangered wildlife. The Forestry Bureau of Yueyang City instituted a civil action incidental to criminal proceedings and requested that the seven defendants should jointly compensate for environmental losses of CNY53,553. The People's Procuratorate of Yueyanglou District supported the action instituted by the Forestry Bureau of Yueyang City.

Influential Environment and Resources Cases in China (2024),
https://doi.org/10.1007/978-981-96-9562-1_2

Judgment

In the trial of first instance, the Primary People's Court of Yueyanglou District of Yueyang City, Hunan Province held that: In collusion with Zhong *jun and Fang *hua, He *qiang illegally killed cygnets, white spoonbills, and other wild animals under state protection (Category II) by poisoning in the Dongtinghu National Nature Reserve in Hunan Province; Li * assisted He *qiang in purchasing pesticides and was fully responsible for selling the wild migratory birds killed by poisoning. The acts of He *qiang, Zhong *jun, Fang *hua, and Li * have constituted a crime of illegal killing of rare and endangered wildlife and the circumstances were particularly serious. Incited by He *qiang, Long *ru, Long *ming, and Long Zhen separately hunted and killed wild migratory birds in the national nature reserve, which damaged wildlife resources. With the serious .circumstances, their acts constituted a crime of illegal hunting. In the meantime, the criminal acts of He *qiang and Zhong *jun constituted a crime of illegal killing of rare and endangered wildlife and a crime of illegal hunting. They should be convicted and punished according to a heavier crime, namely the crime of illegal killing of rare and endangered wildlife. In addition, since the criminal acts of He *qiang and other six persons damaged national wildlife resources and made the national property suffer from damage, all parties should assume the compensation liability. The damage was determined as CNY44,617 according to the verified value of the 63 wild migratory birds involved. On the basis of the different roles of the defendants in the crime, He *qiang, Zhong *jun, Fang *hua, and Li * were sentenced to fixed-term imprisonments ranging from six years to twelve years, in addition to fines for illegal killing of rare and endangered wildlife.

Long *ru, Long *, and Long *ming were sentenced to fixed-term imprisonments ranging from one year and two years and two of them were given probation of two years for illegal hunting. He *qiang and other six persons should jointly pay the Forestry Bureau of Yueyang City CNY44,617 as environmental damage compensation. The Yueyang Intermediate People's Court in Hunan Province rejected the appeal filed by some of the defendants and upheld the judgment of the lower court.

Significance

This is a civil action incidental to criminal proceedings concerning illegal hunting and killing of rare and endangered wildlife. Imposition of a penalty is an important way of environmental governance. With increasingly stern environmental resource problems, using criminal penalties properly can effectively punish environmental and resource crimes and deter future illegal acts as an important link in protecting the ecosystem and the environment. This case took place in the Dongtinghu National Nature Reserve. While the procuratorial organ instituted a public prosecution, the relevant competent department of environmental resources instituted a civil action incidental to criminal proceedings. The procuratorial organ supported the civil action and both the criminal liability and civil liability of the actors were investigated according to the law. The court of the first instance confirmed the intents of all the seven defendants to kill wild migratory birds in the nature reserve by poisoning, and properly distinguished each defendant's role in convicting them of the crime of killing rare and endangered wildlife and the crime of illegal hunting according to the principle of consistency between subjectivity and objectivity; in addition, the court of first instance distinguished principal offenders from accessory offenders according to the theory of joint crime and separately sentenced the seven defendants to fixed-term imprisonments ranging from one year to twelve years and some of them were given a probation, reflecting several basic principles in environmental and criminal law, including severe punishment for environmental and resource related crimes, the independent status of environmental legal interests, and combining punishment with leniency, giving full play to the deterrent and educational functions of the Criminal Law. In addition, in this case, both the criminal liabilities of defendants for killing wild migratory birds and the civil compensation liability for environmental damages were investigated. It is of good exemplary significance for the co-handling of cases concerning environmental resources-related criminal offense and civil compensation.

Courts and Members of the Collegial Bench

Court of First Instance: In Yueyanglou Primary People's Court, Hunan, before Xiao Bingfeng, Li Lin, Wen Jianshe

Court of Second Instance: In Yueyang Intermediate People's Court, Hunan, before Ren Yan, Yu Beibei, et al.

Chapter 3
Civil Public Interest Litigation: Jiangsu ** Environmental Protection Federation v. **Chemicals Company for Water Pollution

Basic Facts

From January 2012 to February 2013, the defendant, Taixing ** chemical company (hereinafter referred to as "the chemical company") and other five enterprises delivered a total of over 25,000 tons of hazardous waste of hydrochloric acid and waste sulfuric acid generated in the process of production to other companies without the qualification for disposal of hazardous wastes at a price ranging from CNY20 to 100 per ton, and such hazardous wastes were directly discharged into Rutai Canal of Taixing City and Gumagan River of Gaogang District, Taizhou City secretly, causing serious water pollution. An environmental protection federation based in Taizhou (hereinafter referred to as "the environmental protection federation") requested the court to order that the six defendant enterprises should pay the environmental restoration fee of over CNY160 million and the appraisal and evaluation fee of CNY100,000.

Judgment

After the trial of first instance, the Intermediate People's Court of Taizhou City of Jiangsu Province held that: as a legally-established non-profit organization engaging in the cause of environmental protection, the environmental protection federation had the standing to institute an environmental public interest litigation. The six defendant enterprises delivered the by-product acid to companies without qualification and capabilities for disposal of such hazardous waste with a much lower cost than the expense needed for legal disposal of such by-product acid, causing the dumping of a great volume of by-product acid into rivers and serious environmental pollution. Therefore, they should compensate for the damage caused thereby and restore the ecosystem and the environment. The dumping of over 20,000 tons of by-product

Influential Environment and Resources Cases in China (2024),
https://doi.org/10.1007/978-981-96-9562-1_3

acid into rivers would inevitably cause serious environmental damage. As the rivers flew, even though the water quality at the location of the dumping took a turn for the better, it did not mean that the environmental status of the rivers have been fully. Under the circumstance where it was difficult to calculate the restoration costs, the ecological and environmental restoration costs should be calculated by adopting the virtual treatment costs method.

Therefore, the court rendered a judgment that the six defendant enterprises should pay the environmental restoration costs of over CNY160 million in total and bear the appraisal and evaluation fee of CNY100,000 and the litigation costs. After the trial of the second instance, the High People's Court of Jiangsu Province confirmed the standing of the environmental protection federation. The court also held that there was clear causation between the disposal of the by-product acid by the six defendant enterprises and the environmental damage in the Gumagan River and Rutai Canal. In the judgment of the first instance, the amount of compensation determined was correct and the method for calculating the restoration costs was appropriate. The six defendant enterprises should legally assume the tortious liability for the damage of environmental pollution caused thereby.

The judgment of the second instance also affirmed that the six defendant enterprises should pay the environmental restoration costs of over CNY160 million but adjusted the methods for performance of obligations—If the six defendant enterprises could make re-use the by-product acids through technical transformation, significantly decrease environmental risks, and received no other environmental punishments within the following year, the technical transformation costs they have paid may be deducted from the environmental restoration costs ordered to be compensated at a share of not more than 40%. Three defendant enterprises have actively performed the entire judgment of second instance. Unsatisfied with the judgment of second instance, the Taixing ** chemical company filed an application for retrial with the Supreme People's Court of the P.R.C.

The Supreme People's Court held that: In cases of environmental pollution, manufacturers of hazardous chemicals and chemical products should perform higher duties of care for their main products and by-products. They should comprehensively understand whether the main products and the by-products generated in the production process were highly hazardous and whether they would cause environmental pollution; they should also be responsible for the manufacturing, sale, transportation, storage, and disposal of their main products to be compliant with the relevant legal provisions, and avoid damage to the environment, including major risks of environmental damage. Although rivers flow and have the capabilities of self-purification, the environmental capacity of one certain river is limited. The dumping of a large volume of by-product acid to water bodies would inevitably cause severe damage to the water quality, aquatic animals and plants in rivers, riverbeds, river banks, and the ecosystem in the downstream rivers. If the restoration failed to be made in a timely manner, the accumulation of pollutants would inevitably exceed the environmental carrying capacity and finally cause irreversible environmental damage.

Therefore, the polluters should not be exempted from liability of environmental restoration on the ground that the water quality of part of the water areas had been restored. The Supreme People's Court finally ruled to deny the chemical company's application for retrial.

Significance

This case was described as an environmental public interest litigation case of "sky-high" compensation in the media. In this case, a social organization served as plaintiff, the procuratorial organ upheld the action. The case involved a mix of parties, multiple defendants, high amount of compensation determined, as well as explorations and innovations, so is of high reference value. The court of the first instance properly identified the standing of the environmental protection federation as the plaintiff, and determined that the chemical company and other five companies had the subjective intention of illegally disposing of hazardous wastes, objectively caused the consequence of serious environmental pollution, and should assume the liability of compensation for environmental damage and restoration. At the same time, in light of the appraisal conclusion and the expert opinions, the court of the first instance determined the environmental restoration costs, and ordered that the six defendant enterprises should compensate the total environmental restoration costs of over CNY160 million. The court of second instance balanced the needs for survival and development of enterprises and goal of environmental protection, innovated in the payment method of restoration costs, and encouraged enterprises to make more efforts in technical upgrade and assume their subject liability and social liability for environmental protection, properly handled the relations between overall interests and partial interests and between long-term interests and short-term interests. The Supreme People's Court affirmed the court of second instance's innovation in the payment method of restoration costs, encouraged enterprises to actively carry out technical innovations and upgrade, and promoted the improvement of regional ecological and environmental quality. In the meantime, the Supreme People's Court specified that the manufacturers of hazardous chemicals and chemical products should perform higher duties of care in the process of manufacturing and assume more social liability. For river water, an environmental medium with fluidity and self-purification capability, the Supreme People's Court determined the treatment principle of water restoration. In other words, once pollution occurred, the restoration obligations assumed by the polluter should not be affected by the self-improvement of the water environment. This case was of demonstration significance in the handling of water pollution cases.

Courts and Members of the Collegial Bench

Court of First Instance: In Taixing Intermediate People's Court, Jiangsu, before Ji Alin, Ye Zhijun, Cai Peng, Wang Jianxiang, Wang Yaguang

Court of Second Instance: In Jiangsu High People's Court, before Liu Jiangong, Chen Ying, et al.

Retrial: In Supreme People's Court, before Lin Wenxue, Wei Wenchao, Liu Xiaofei, Wu Kaimin, et al.

Chapter 4
Series Civil Public Interest Litigation: China ** Environmental Protection Foundation v. Ningxia ** Technology Company for Tengger Desert Pollution

Basic Facts

On August 8, 2015, the China **Environmental Protection Foundation (hereinafter referred to as the "the Foundation") filed an action in the Intermediate People's Court of Zhongwei City of Ningxia Hui Autonomous Region and alleged that: in the process of production, Ningxia ** technology company and other seven enterprises directly discharged sewage exceeding the prescribed standards to the evaporation pond in violation of regulations, causing severe pollution of the Tengger Desert. Up to the time of action, the rectification had not been completed yet. The Foundation requested the Court to order that the technology company should (1) stop the illegal environmental pollution activities; (2) eliminate hazards causing the environmental pollution; (3) restore the ecology and environment or establish a special fund for the restoration and entrust a qualified third party to implement the restoration; (4) with respect to claims in items (2) and (3), it was requested that the Court should organize the plaintiff, technical experts, legal experts, NPC members, and CPPCC members to jointly review the elimination and the restoration results; (5) compensate for the ecological function loss until full restoration; and (6) extend a formal apology on national media. The Foundation submitted to the Court its legal registration certificate, which showed that it is a foundation legal person registered with the Ministry of Civil Affairs of the People's Republic of China. The annual review materials from 2010 to 2014 submitted by the Foundation demonstrated that it passed the annual inspections in five consecutive years before filing the public interest litigation. The Foundation also submitted a statement that it had no records of administrative or criminal penalty within the recent five years. Besides, the charter of the Foundation provided that mission is to "widely mobilize the whole society to care and support the cause of biodiversity protection and green development, protect the national strategic resources, promote the building of ecological civilization and harmony between man and nature, and build a better home for humanity." The Foundation also submitted to the Court the relevant evidentiary materials that since its establishment in 1985,

Influential Environment and Resources Cases in China (2024),
https://doi.org/10.1007/978-981-96-9562-1_4

it has been engaged in such activities as hosting environmental protection seminars, organizing ecological fieldtrips, launching publicity and education campaigns for environmental protection, and filing civil environmental public interest litigation cases.

Judgment

In the trial of first instance, the Intermediate People's Court of Zhongwei City of Ningxia Hui Autonomous Region held that the Foundation could not be deemed as a social organization "specially engaging in the public activities of environmental protection" as prescribed in Article 58 of the Environmental Protection Law. Therefore, it ruled that the foundation had no standing to file the action. The Foundation refused to accept the ruling and appealed. After examination, the High People's Court of Ningxia Hui Autonomous Region ruled to dismiss the appeal and affirmed the original ruling. The Foundation then filed an application for retrial with the Supreme People's Court of the P.R.C. The Supreme People's Court, in accordance with the law, brought the case to trial and held that: since environmental public interests are inclusive and sharable, it is impossible to determine one specific direct interested party legally. It is therefore necessary to encourage, guide, and regulate social organizations to file environmental public interest litigation in accordance with the law, so as to better bring the functions of environmental public interest litigation into play. In accordance with the provisions of Article 58 of the Environmental Protection Law and Article 4 of the Interpretation of the Supreme People's Court on Several Issues concerning the Application of Law in the Trial of Environmental Civil Public Interests Litigations (hereinafter referred to as the "Interpretation"), the issue of whether the Foundation involved in this case could file an action as a social organization "specially engaged in public activities of environmental protection" should be examined mainly from three aspects, namely whether its missions and business scope included safeguarding the environmental public interests, whether it actually engaged in public activities of environmental protection, and whether the environmental public interests it safeguarded were related to its missions and business scope. Whether the missions and business scope of a social organization included safeguarding the environmental public interests should be judged according to the content and nature of its work other than just the literal expression. Even though the charter of a social organization did not specifically contain the wording "safeguarding the environmental public interests," if the work content was within the scope of protecting various natural elements impacting the survival and development of mankind and those subject to artificial modification, it should be identified that the missions and business scope of the organization included safeguarding the environmental public interests. The missions in the charter of the Foundation aligned with green development and were closely related to environmental protection, and should be deemed to be within the scope of safeguarding the environmental public interests. Public activities of environmental protection not only include activities directly improving the environment such as tree planting, protection of endangered species, energy conservation and emission reduction, and environmental restoration, but also environmental protection—related publicity and education, research and training, academic exchange, legal aid, public interest litigation, and other activities that were conducive to improving the environmental governance system, enhancing the environmental management capacity, and promoting public consensus on environmental protection in the whole society. Although the relevant evidentiary materials submitted by the Foundation in the trial of first instance, second instance, and retrial was not cross-examined, including the history of the organization, photographs of public activities, and notice on case-filing and acceptance of previous environmental public interest litigation cases, at the stage of case-filing and examination, they were sufficient enough to show that since its establishment in 1985, the Foundation has been actually engaged in environmental protection activities, including hosting environmental protection seminars, organizing ecological fieldtrips, launching publicity and education campaigns on environmental protection, and filing environmental civil public interest litigation, for a long time and was in complaint with the provisions of the Environmental Protection Law and the Interpretation. In the meantime, the aforesaid evidence also proved that the duration in which the Foundation engaged in public activities of environmental protection has been over five years and was in line with the provisions on standings of Article 58 of the Environmental Protection Law that a social organization eligible for civil environmental public interest litigation should engage in public activities of environmental protection for five consecutive years or more. In accordance with the provisions of Article 4 of the Interpretation, the public environmental interests involved in the public interest litigation filed by a social organization should have certain relevance with the missions and business scope of the social organization. Even though the matter instituted by the social organization did not have a direct co-relationship with the missions and business scope of the social organization, if such matter had certain relevance with the environmental elements or the ecological system under the protection of the social organization, the standing of the social organization should be confirmed according to the standard of relevance. This environmental public interest litigation was filed due to pollution of the Tengger Desert. The complex and fragile desert ecological system formed in the interaction between desert biocenosis and the environment required much more cherishment and good care of the mankind during utilization. In the action, the Foundation alleged that the technology company discharged sewage exceeding the prescribed standards to the evaporation pond, which severely damaged the already fragile ecological system of the Tengger Desert. Safeguarding the environmental public interests involved was included in the missions and business scope of the Foundation. In addition, the foundation's legal person registration certificate, the annual review materials, and the statement on no penalty records submitted by the Foundation showed that it matched other requirements for social organizations to file environmental public interest litigation as prescribed in Article 58 of the Environmental Protection Law and Articles 2, 3, and 5 of the Interpretation, and the Foundation had the standing for filing a civil environmental public interest litigation. The Supreme People's Court rendered a retrial ruling to set aside the rulings of the first and second instance and ordered the Intermediate People's Court of Zhongwei City to place the case on file for hearing.

Significance

Through the trial of a series of civil public interest litigation over pollution of the Tengger Desert and handling the prominent issues related to the standing of plaintiff in the trial of environmental public interest litigation cases in various regions since the implementation of the newly-revised Environmental Protection Law, the Supreme People's Court determined and described the judicial rules for the application of law regarding the standing of plaintiff as prescribed in Article 58 of the Environmental Protection Law and the Interpretation. It was specified in the retrial ruling that in respect of the standing of a social organization in filing a civil environmental public interest litigation, the social organization should be examined mainly from three aspects, namely whether its missions and business scope included safeguarding the environmental public interests, whether it actually was engaged in public activities of environmental protection, and whether the environmental public interests it safeguarded in the case involved were related to its missions and business scope. The ruling elaborated that whether the missions and business scope of a social organization included safeguarding the environmental public interests should be judged by the contents of the organization's work other than literal wordings; that public activities of environmental protection not only included activities of directly improving the environment, but also activities conducive to improving the environmental governance system, enhancing the environmental management capabilities, and promoting public consensus on environmental protection; and that even though the matter instituted by the social organization did not have direct co-relation with its missions and business scope, if such matter had certain relevance with the environmental elements or the ecological system under the protection of the social organization, the standing of the social organization should also be affirmed according to the standard of relevance. In this series of cases, the Supreme People's Court specified the standards for standing in civil environmental public interest litigation at the judicial level for the first time, promoted the development of the environmental public interest litigation system. These cases have been published by the Supreme People's Court as guiding cases and served as demonstration for future trials of cases of similar nature.

Court and Members of the Collegial Bench

Retrial: In Supreme People's Court, before Liu Xiaofei, Ye Yang, Wu Kaimin

Chapter 5
Civil Public Interest Litigation: Beijing Chaoyang ** Environmental Research Institute, Fujian ** Environmental Center v. Xie *jin and Three Other Persons for Deforestation

Basic Facts

On July 29, 2008, Xie *jin and three others expanded mining outside the area authorized by competent authorities. By stripping away the vegetation of the mountain from top down, dumping the abandoned rocks generated by mining down the mountain, and building a shed under the mine, the defendants seriously destroyed 28.33 mu of woodland vegetation. On July 28, 2014, Xie *jin et al. were sentenced to imprisonment for the crime of illegally occupying agricultural land. On January 1, 2015, the Beijing Chaoyang ** Environmental Research Institute and Fujian ** Environmental Center filed a lawsuit, requesting that the four defendants be ordered to restore the forest land vegetation within certain time frame and compensate for the loss of ecological and environmental service functions in the amount of CNY 1.34 million; if the forest land vegetation cannot be restored timely, the defendants shall also pay for the cost of environmental damage restoration of over CNY 1.1 million; they shall also jointly reimburse the plaintiffs for the environmental damage assessment fee, attorney's fee, and other reasonable costs incurred in the proceeding.

Judgment

Fujian Nanping Intermediate People's Court held in the first instance that Xie *jin and three others occupied forest land for mining, which not only seriously damaged the vegetation of 28.33 mu of forest land, but also caused the loss of ecological services during the period from the damage of forest vegetation to the restoration to the baseline state. Therefore, Xie *jin and other three persons were ordered to restore the function of the damaged 28.33 mu of forest land within five months from the effective date of the judgment, reforest the land and nurture, and conserve the saplings for three years; if failing to do so, they shall jointly compensate for the

Influential Environment and Resources Cases in China (2024),
https://doi.org/10.1007/978-981-96-9562-1_5

environmental damage restoration costs of more than CNY 1.1 million and loss of ecological service function of CNY 1.27 million for in situ or off-site ecological restoration; they shall also jointly pay the plaintiff the appraisal fee, attorney's fee, and other reasonable expenses for the litigation of over CNY 165,000. The Fujian High People's Court upheld the verdict of the first instance.

Significance

This case is the first national civil environmental public interest litigation since the revised Environmental Protection Law came into force, it involved the review of the plaintiff's eligibility to sue, the liability for environmental restoration, and the compensation for the loss of ecological and environmental service functions. In accordance with Article 58 of the Environmental Protection Law of the People's Republic of China and the Interpretation of the Supreme People's Court on Several Issues concerning the Application of Law to the Adjudication of Environmental Civil Public Interest Litigation, the court handed down a judgment confirming the standing of the institute and the center to bring the public interest litigation case. The court of the first instance prioritized ecological restoration, ordering the defendants to restore the function of the damaged forest land within a timeframe, reforest the land and nurture, and conserve the saplings for three years. The ultimate purpose of restoring the vegetation and the damaged ecosystem is thus fulfilled. The decision has set a precedent by supporting the request for compensation for the loss of service function during the period from when the damage happened till the restoration of land to the baseline state. It raised the cost of ecological damage and highlighted the values of environmental protection.

Courts and Members of the Collegial Bench

Court of First Instance: In Nanping Intermediate People's Court, FuJian, before Lin Dongbo, Gan Daixing, Zhang Tinggui, Huang Huiqin, Zhu Feng

Court of Second Instance: In Fujian High People's Court, before Zhu Changlin, Li Heping, Lin Jinbin

Chapter 6
Civil Public Interest Litigation: Jiangsu Xuzhou People's Procuratorate v. Xuzhou ** Papermaking Company for Water Pollution

Basic Facts

The local competent department of environmental protection found multiple times that Xuzhou ** Papermaking Company (hereinafter referred to as "the papermaking company") discharged production sewage to the Subei Dike River connecting to the Beijing-Hangzhou Canal through privately-set subsurface drainage pipes. The chemical oxygen demand (COD), ammonia nitrogen, total phosphorus, and other pollutant indicators in the sewage exceeded the prescribed standards. Previously, the Environmental Protection Bureau of Tongshan District, Xuzhou City, Jiangsu Province had imposed administrative penalties on the papermaking company twice. On December 28, 2015, as a public interest litigant, the People's Procuratorate of Xuzhou City instituted civil environmental public interest litigation in the Intermediate People's Court of Xuzhou City and requested the Court to order that the papermaking company should restore the environment of the Subei Dike River damaged by the pollution to the original state and compensate for the service function losses during the period from when the damage happened until the full restoration of the river to the original state; if the papermaking company could not restore the environment to the original state, the People's Procuratorate of Xuzhou City requested the Court to order that the company should assume the liability of compensation to pay a cost three to five times of the benchmark restoration cost (benchmark cost: CNY 269,100 per 2600 tons).

Influential Environment and Resources Cases in China (2024),
https://doi.org/10.1007/978-981-96-9562-1_6

Judgment

In the trial of first instance, the Intermediate People's Court of Xuzhou City of Jiangsu Province held that: The discharge of sewage by the papermaking company had caused environmental pollution, and the company should assume the liability for environmental pollution. Considering the facts of environmental pollution caused, the intent of the papermaking company, the operation costs of pollution prevention and control facilities, the service functions of the ecological environment, and the difficulty in ecological restoration, the costs for ecological restoration from the damage happened till full restoration that should be borne by the papermaking company could be calculated based on the ecological function loss during the period. Therefore, the Court rendered a judgment that papermaking company should pay a total of CNY1.0582 million as ecological damage compensation. The papermaking company appealed upon the judgment against the People's Procuratorate of Xuzhou City, public interest litigant in the trial of the first instance. In the trial of the second instance, the High People's Court of Jiangsu Province held that: The fact that the environmental quality of the sewage discharge point has reached the required standard could not serve as the ground for the papermaking company's refusal to bear the cost for ecological restoration. It was not inappropriate for the judgment of the first instance to use 2.035 times as the coefficient in the calculation of the restoration costs based on the method of virtual treatment costs. There were both factual basis and legal basis to use four times of the volume of sewage discharged for the calculation of the environmental restoration costs. The Court rendered a judgment of the second instance to dismiss the appeal and affirm the original judgment.

Significance

This case is among the first batch of civil public interest litigation accepted by the people's courts since the Standing Committee of the National People's Congress authorized procuratorial organs to initiate the pilot program of filing public interest litigation and it is also the first case of second instance tried by the people's court where the procuratorial organ initiated the pilot program of instituting public interest litigation. The court of the first instance also attached importance to information disclosure and public participation during the trial. The collegial bench consisted of judges and people's jurors and the court session was live broadcasted to the public in video and texts. During the court hearings, expert witness were invited to raise expert opinions on technical issues, helping the court to make impartial and science-based decisions in environmental cases. In this case, the ecological restoration costs was reasonably determined considering factors including the degree of subjective fault of defendant for its illegal discharge of pollutants, the concealment of its pollutant discharge activities, and the environmental damage consequences. Through the judgment, the costs of law-violation for the polluting enterprise were increased, deterring the illegal discharge of pollutants by the enterprise from the source. In accordance with the Civil Procedure Law and the Decision of the Standing Committee of the National People's Congress on Authorizing the Supreme People's Procuratorate to Launch the Pilot Program of Filing Public Interest Litigations in Some Areas, the court of the second instance tried the case and demonstrated how the rules for such cases function.

Courts and Members of the Collegial Bench

Court of First Instance: In Xuzhou Intermediate People's Court, Jiangsu, before Cai Keyong, Li Juan, Chen Hu, Xu Shuqi, Zhou Xiaoyun

Court of Second Instance: In Jiangsu High People's Court, before Chen Ying, Zang Jing, Zhao Li

Chapter 7
Civil Public Interest Litigation: ** Environment Protection Federation v. Dezhou ** Company for Air Pollution

Basic Facts

Domiciled in Dezhou City, Shandong Province, Dezhou ** Co., Ltd. (hereinafter referred to as "** Company") was an enterprise engaging in the manufacturing of glass and highly-processed glass products. Although ** Company invested in the construction of desulfurization and dust removal facilities, there was still constant emission of pollutants exceeding the prescribed standards through two chimneys, causing air pollution and seriously affecting the lives of surrounding residents. It was criticized by the Ministry of Environmental Protection by name and repeatedly penalized by the competent administrative department of environmental protection, but the illegal emission. **Environment Protection Federation (hereinafter referred to as "the Federation") instituted an action in the Intermediate People's Court of Dezhou City and requested the Court to order that ** Company should immediately cease the emission of pollutants to the air exceeding the prescribed standards and add more air pollution prevention and control facilities, and should not resume the production and operation until such facilities passed the review and acceptance of the competent environmental authorities and were put into use; ** Company should pay CNY20.4 million (changed to CNY27.46 million during litigation) as compensation for the damage caused by the excessive emission of pollutants and CNY7.8 million for losses caused by its refusal to correct.

The aforesaid sums of money should be paid to the special financial account of the local government for air pollution control in Dezhou City; ** Company should extend a formal apology to the public on the media at or above the provincial level; and ** Company should bear the litigation fee, inspection fee, appraisal fee, expert witness fee, lawyers' fee, and other expenses involved in the litigation. After accepting the case, the Intermediate People's Court of Dezhou City of Shandong Province served the complaint for civil action and other materials on claim upon ** Company, made a public announcement on the case-filing, and informed the Environmental Protection

Influential Environment and Resources Cases in China (2024),
https://doi.org/10.1007/978-981-96-9562-1_7

Bureau of Dezhou City. The People's Government of Dezhou City and the Environmental Protection Bureau of Dezhou City actively supported the trial of this case, and jointly held coordination meetings with the court of the first instance. Through the cooperation and coordination between the judicial organ and the competent administrative department of environmental protection, ** Company closed down all production lines, selected a new site in Tianqu Industrial Park far away from living quarters for residents, and constructed a new plant. In this way, further expansion of pollution and damage was contained and interim measures were taken during the trial of the case when the case was still pending.

Judgment

In the trial of first instance, the Intermediate People's Court of Dezhou City of Shandong Province held that during litigation, ** Company drew off the water, suspended production, and ceased the use of the original plant. Hence it may be deemed that ** Company has ceased infringement. Before ceasing the emission of pollutants, ** Company had not been equipped with or had not run desulfuration and denitration facilities, had not been equipped with dust removal facilities or had had dust removal facilities with insufficient processing capacity, and repeatedly emitted such pollutants as sulfur dioxide, nitric oxide, and smoke and dust to the air exceeding the prescribed standards. In particular, sulfur dioxide and nitric oxide were precursors to acid rain. The acid rain formed by the excessive emission of sulfur dioxide and nitric oxide would bring personal injury and property damage to residents and the excessive emission of smoke and dust would affect the atmospheric visibility and air cleanliness. Since ** Company's excessive emission of pollutants resulted in damage to the ecologic added-value of atmospheric environment, it should be liable for ecological and environmental restoration and compensate for losses of service functions during the period from the time when the damage happened to its restoration to the original state. In the meantime, ** Company's excessive emission of pollutants to the atmosphere infringed upon the benefits and interests of the public and it should assume the civil liability for extending a formal apology. Therefore, the Intermediate People's Court of Dezhou City rendered a judgment that ** Company should pay CNY21.9836 million as compensation for losses caused by its excessive emission of pollutants, which would be used for the atmospheric environmental quality restoration; and ** Company should extend a formal apology to the public on the media at or above the provincial level. After the judgment of first instance was pronounced, no party appealed and the judgment has come into force.

Significance

The case in Dezhou City is the first public interest litigation case on air pollution in the Beijing-Tianjin-Hebei region and surrounding regions accepted by the people's court since the implementation of the revised Environmental Protection Law. With mobility, the atmosphere itself has certain self-purification functions. The difficulty in the trial of this case was whether an enterprise's excessive emission of pollutants constituted damage to the environment. The judgment of this case specified that the excessive emission of sulfur dioxide, nitric oxide, and dust would affect the ecological service functions of the atmosphere and the emitting enterprise should bear legal liability. The virtual costs of air pollution control may be calculated according to the volume of pollutants emitted by exceeding the prescribed standards and the unit control costs of sulfur dioxide, nitric oxide, and dust and the virtual costs served as basis for compensation for ecological and environmental damage. It was worth approving that during litigation, ** Company voluntarily assumed social responsibility and actively adopted measures to prevent the continuity and expansion of pollution. The conclusion of this case responded to the public concerns over the air pollution control in the Beijing-Tianjin-Hebei region and the surrounding regions in a timely manner and demonstrated a good practice for the control of regional air pollution.

Court and Members of the Collegial Bench

Court of First Instance: In Dezhou Intermediate People's Court, Shandong, before Liu Libing, Zhang Xiaoxue, Gao Xiaomin

Chapter 8
Case of Contractual Disputes: Sichuan ** Mining Company v. Xinjiang **Resource Investment Company Over Mineral Rights

Basic Facts

On October 10, 2011, Xinjiang ** Resource Investment Company (hereinafter referred to as "the investment company") signed a "Cooperative Exploration and Development Agreement" (hereinafter referred to as "the Agreement" with Sichuan ** Mining Company (hereinafter referred to as "the mining company"). It was agreed that the two parties would jointly establish a project company and that the mining company would transfer its exploration rights to the project company when conditions were met at a cost of CNY 35 million compensated by the investment company. Following the agreement, the investment company made the payment of CNY 35 million to the mining company on October 25, 2011. Then on November 22, 2013, the investment company requested to cancel the Agreement on the grounds that the area for cooperative mining exploration was situated in the Tashkurgan Wildlife Nature Reserve in Xinjiang, and the request was declined by the mining company. In order to establish the legality of the Agreement and the invalidity of the request for termination of the contract by the investment company, the mining company filed a lawsuit. The investment company, on the other hand, filed a counterclaim, requesting to cancel the Agreement and that the mining company to return the payment of CNY 35 million and compensate for other losses incurred.

Judgment

The High People's Court of Xinjiang Uygur Autonomous Region in its first instance dismissed the investment company's claims, deciding that the request of the investing company to cancel the Agreement was invalid, and that both parties should continue to implement the Agreement. The Supreme People's Court however, in the second instance, held that the mining exploration right of the mining company involved the

Influential Environment and Resources Cases in China (2024),
https://doi.org/10.1007/978-981-96-9562-1_8

Tashkurgan Wildlife Nature Reserve, which had been created before the exploration right of the mining company was granted. Both parties were or should have been aware that the exploration and exploitation of mineral resources were prohibited in nature reserves, according the Cooperative Exploration and Development Agreement. The Agreement was in violation of the restrictive rules of China's Regulation on Nature Reserve. The natural environment, ecology, and the general public's environmental interests and benefits would suffer significantly if the Agreement were determined to be valid and continued to be in effect. Therefore, in accordance with the law, the contract should be void, and the CNY 35 million in cooperative remuneration that the mining company has already received should be returned. As for the compensation for other losses requested by the investment company, part should be covered by the mining company at a reasonable discount, part should be borne by the investment company itself or be resolved after the liquidation of the project company. The decision of the first instance court was overturned.

Significance

The conflicts between the needs for environmental conservation and economic development are more frequently seen in special ecosystems such as nature reserves, scenic spots, important ecological functioning areas, eco-environmental sensitive areas, and fragile areas. In hearing and enforcing cases in such areas, the court should adopt different measures, taking into full consideration of the different roles of different functional areas according to the national and provincial land and spatial planning. Priority should be given to the environment's capacity in developing the economy, and in particular, for environmental disputes in areas where development is prohibited or restricted, such as the ecological redline areas, the most stringent protection measures should be put in place. Any mining exploration and exploitation contracts involving the aforementioned areas should be under strict scrutiny of the people's courts, regardless of the approval for the contract from the competent land and resource departments. The contract shall be deemed void if it contravenes with existing laws and harms public interests. The ruling of the case sets a precedent for the trial of validity of contracts involving development and utilization of natural resources.

Court and Members of the Collegial Bench

Court of Second Instance: In Supreme People's Court, before Wang Jijun, Yan Jing, Zhu Jing

Chapter 9
Case of Damage Compensation: Guizhou ** Eco-Farming and Development Company v. Guizhou ** Aluminum Industry Company for Property Damage Compensation

Basic Facts

Sturgeon farming is the core business of Guizhou ** Eco-farming and Development Company (hereinafter referred to as "the farming company"). The company uses water from the Gojiazhai Ditch for farming. In October 2014, Guizhou ** Aluminium Industry Company (hereinafter referred to as "the aluminum company"), constructed a dam to draw water from the Gojiazhai Reservoir's in the upstream. The construction of the dam caused the drop of water quantity of the downstream, affecting the farming company's sturgeon ponds—a considerable number of sturgeon raised by the farming company perished because of severe water shortage and oxygen deprivation between April 21 and 23. The farming company asserted that the aluminum company, in constructing the dam, should have taken adequate remediation measures given its knowledge of the potential impacts to water supply. However in reality, the aluminum company stored water without permission and turned off the water supply for downstream without prior notice, killing sturgeons in large quantity. The farming company filed a lawsuit against the aluminum company before the court, alleging that the aluminum company should be liable for compensation.

Judgment

The Qingzhen Primary People's Court of Guizhou Province ruled in the first instance that, the ecological flows of rivers can guarantee the capacity of the rivers for self-purification diffusion, preserve the balance of aquatic ecosystems, and provide the water quality and quantity needed by the aquaculture sector in the reservoir area. Although there is no specific rules for ecological flow in China's law, it is necessary to ensure the minimum discharge flow of hydropower plants in practice. The aluminum company used the water by building the dam without a valid administrative permit

Influential Environment and Resources Cases in China (2024),
https://doi.org/10.1007/978-981-96-9562-1_9

for water-taking and proper environmental impact assessment, causing the shortage of ecological flow, leading to decrease in water flow downstream and in the water intake of the sturgeon aqua farm, resulting in suffocation of sturgeons in the pond. The causation between the mortality of the sturgeon raised by the farming company and the water storage of the aluminum company could be established, and the aluminum firm should make up for the farming company's economic loss of CNY 757,158.6. The aluminum company appealed and was dismissed by the Guiyang Intermediate People's Court. The original verdict was maintained.

Significance

The Yangtze River basin is abundant with water resources. Thus it is a crucial responsibility of the people's courts to hear matters related to Yangtze River protection and sustainable use in accordance with the law. This case involves the protection and regulation of "ecological flow" in using water resources. It is an infringement dispute resulting from the process of developing and utilizing water resources. Rivers' ecological flow is of significant importance. Water users in upstream areas should protect river ecological flow during the development and use of water resources and should not infringe on the legal rights and interests of downstream beneficiaries of ecological flow in water supply, navigation, irrigation, and breeding. It is necessary to maintain the core functions of aquatic ecosystems throughout the entire basin. In this instance, two companies—a sturgeon farm and an aluminum company—are water users of the Gojiazhai Reservoir and should take, use, and discharge water in line with the legislation. The aluminum company should be held legally liable for compensation if it damages the legitimate rights and interests of downstream water users by building interception dams illegally in the upper reaches without water taking and using permits the environmental impact assessment. This decision of the court upholds the importance of ecological flow and protects the legitimate rights and interests of ecological flow beneficiaries, providing guidance for the people's courts in hearing disputes involving water use.

Courts and Members of the Collegial Bench

Court of First Instance: In Qingzhen Primary People's Court, Guizhou, before Luo Guangqian, Li Yunhe, Zhang Qi

Court of Second Instance: In Guiyang Intermediate People's Court, Guizhou, before Zeng Zhen, Tang Yuping, Ma Jie

Chapter 10
Case of Hainan ** Water Company v. Hainan ** Environmental Protection Bureau Over Administrative Penalty

Basic Facts

The Environmental Protection Bureau of Danzhou City held that Hainan ** Water Co., Ltd. (hereinafter referred to as the "** Water Company") was suspected of illegally discharging water pollutant based on a monitoring report issued by the Environmental Monitoring Center of Hainan Province on June 5, 2013 (hereinafter referred to as "No. 153 Monitoring Report"). On April 16, 2014, Danzhou Environmental Protection Bureau issued a warning for administrative penalty to the ** Water Company. Within the statutory time limit, the ** Water Company failed to file an application for a statement of explanation, defending itself, or holding a hearing. As a result, on June 16 of the same year, the Environmental Protection Bureau of Danzhou City issued a Written Decision on Administrative Penalty (No. 47 [2014], Environmental Protection, Danzhou) (hereinafter referred to as the "No. 47 Penalty Decision") requesting ** Water Company should pay a fine of CNY177,719, two times of the regular costs for sewage. Upon reconsideration, the People's Government of Danzhou City affirmed the No. 47 Penalty Decision.

The ** Water Company refused to accept the penalty decision and appealed to the Primary People's Court of Danzhou City, requesting the revocation of the No. 47 Penalty Decision.

Judgment

In the trial of first instance, the People's Court of Danzhou City of Hainan Province held that: As the competent administrative department of environmental protection in Danzhou City, the Environmental Bureau of Danzhou City had the statutory functions of imposing an administrative penalty on any entity that illegally discharged water

Influential Environment and Resources Cases in China (2024),
https://doi.org/10.1007/978-981-96-9562-1_10

pollutants. In accordance with the provisions of Article 34 of the Measures for Environmental Administrative Penalty, sampling was a mandatory procedure of monitoring in this case. However, the Environmental Protection Bureau of Danzhou City failed to provide the sampling record, sampling process, and other relevant evidence and failed to testify the authenticity of the submitted samples, which directly affected the authenticity of the monitoring results. In this case, the Environmental Protection Bureau of Danzhou City failed to collect conclusive evidence for proving the authentic and reliable source of samples, and determined that the ** Water Company discharged excessive sewage only on the basis of the result of the No. 153 Monitoring Report. The main evidence for the decision was insufficient. On June 16, 2014, the Environmental Protection Bureau of Danzhou City imposed another fine on the ** Water Company for its excessive discharge of sewage on January 14 and May 22, 2013. The decision was procedurally illegal. In the No. 47 Penalty Decision, the ** Water Company was only ordered to pay a fine and it was not ordered to make corrections within a prescribed time limit. The administrative penalty was obviously improper. The court of the first instance rendered a judgment that the No. 47 Penalty Decision should be set aside and the Environmental Protection Bureau of Danzhou City should bear the litigation costs. In the trial of the second instance, the Second Intermediate People's Court of Hainan Province held that: The legality of the No. 153 Monitoring Report was the foundation for examining whether the fact-finding in the administrative penalty was clear. Since the sampling procedure in the No. 153 Monitoring Report was illegal, it could not serve as the material evidence for the decision that the ** Water Company committed any environmental violations. Except for the No. 153 Monitoring Report, the Environmental Protection Bureau did not conduct any other investigations and it violated the provisions on separation of investigation and punishment. The procedure was illegal. The material evidence based on which the facts were found in the No. 47 Penalty Decision was insufficient and the application of law was erroneous. The court of the second instance rendered a judgment to dismiss the appeal and affirm the original judgment.

Significance

This is a case concerning dispute over an environmental administrative penalty and involves examination and determination for the environmental penalty. It is a model case with guiding significance. In recent years, the administrative law enforcement departments of environmental protection at various levels have exerted more efforts to administrative law enforcement of environmental violations and effectively contained environmental pollution. However, seen from the cases heard by the court relating to environmental administrative penalties, sometimes the procedures for such enforcement decisions are flawed. The problem of "emphasis of results over procedures" exists. In environmental monitoring, the environmental law enforcement department should attach importance to the procedures. In particular, in cases concerning penalties for water pollution, the technical specifications for sampling directly affects the validity of the testing results. Therefore, the Measures for Environmental Administrative Penalty specifically provided procedures for investigation and sampling on site—it is necessary to keep the sampling records or the sampling process should be included in inspection reports. The sampling may be recorded by photographs, recording, and other means. Since the Environmental Protection Bureau of Danzhou City failed to provide the sampling record, the sampling process, and other relevant evidence and failed to prove the legality of its sampling procedure, the people's court determined that the No. 153 Monitoring Report could not serve as the material evidence for the fact that the ** Water Company had environmental violations and the No. 47 Penalty Decision should be revoked according to the law. The judgment of this case demonstrated supervision of the people's court over environmental administrative law enforcement and it plays a positive role in promoting the competent environmental administrative authorities in exercising the administrative penalty in a standardized manner, contributing to law-based administration.

Courts and Members of the Collegial Bench

Court of First Instance: In Danzhou Primary People's Court, Hainan, before Wang Qinghua, Wang Bo, Liu Yaoxiong

Court of Second Instance: In Hainan Second Intermediate People's Court, Hainan, before Zhang Dexiong, Wen Kuixing, Liu Xia

Chapter 11
Environmental Pollution Case Against Deqing Minghe Insulation Material Co., Ltd. and Qi ** for Illegal Use of Controlled ODS

Keywords Criminal · Environment pollution · International environmental treaties · Unlawful use of controlled ozone-depleting substances (ODS) · Other harmful substances

Basic Facts

Deqing Minghe Insulation Material Co., Ltd. (hereinafter referred to as Minghe), founded on March 8, 2017, is in the business of manufacturing rigid polyurethane (PU) foam (combined polyether) insulation materials and wholesaling and retailing of polyurethane insulation materials, chemical raw materials (excluding hazardous chemicals and easily-made toxic chemicals), plastics and construction materials. Between August 2017 and June 2019, the company's legal representative, QI **, purchased Trichlorofluoromethane (CFC-11) from Li **, Han **, Ge **, and Xue ** whom were charged in separate proceedings for foam manufacturing. The defendant conducted the purchasing act in the knowledge that CFC-11 was a controlled ozone-depleting substance (ODS) explicitly banned in production. During that period, Minghe acquired a total of 849.5 tons of CFC-11. According to Qi's statement and the witness testimony, Minghe produced and sold at least 2427 tons of rigid PU foam insulation materials containing CFC-11. The calculations of the Hangzhou Research Institute of China Coal Technology and Engineering Group showed that the emissions estimated associated with Minghe's use of CFC-11 in manufacturing was 30,410 kg. According to Deqing Tianqin Accounting Firm Co., the earnings per ton of rigid PU foam containing CFC-11 was CNY 602.1, which placed Minghe's total unlawful revenue at CNY 1,461,296.7 (2427 tons * CNY 602.1/ton).

CFC-11 is completely banned as Type I CFCs in China's List of Controlled Ozone Depleting Substances jointly issued by the Ministry of Ecology and Environment (formerly the Ministry of Environmental Protection), the National Development and

Influential Environment and Resources Cases in China (2024),
https://doi.org/10.1007/978-981-96-9562-1_11

Reform Commission, and the Ministry of Industry and Information Technology on September 27, 2010.

On October 23, 2019, the Ecological and Environmental Bureau of Huzhou, Zhejiang, issued a decision letter on administrative penalties (HD Env. Penalty No. [2019] 59), imposing a fine of CNY 200,000 on Minghe for storing pentane and other chemicals in containerized coolers and warehouses for production purpose in violation of the EIA requirements. On the same day, the Ecological and Environmental Bureau issued another decision letter on environmental administrative penalty (HD Env. Penalty No. [2019] 60) to fine Minghe CNY 500,000 for unpermitted use of ODS in production.

Judgment

According to the ruling (No. 592 [2019] First, Criminal, 592, Zhejiang) made by the People's Court of Deqing, Zhejiang on March 6, 2020, 1. Minghe, guilty of polluting the environment is fined CNY 700,000 (paid within 30 days after the judgment takes effect; the fines imposed via the administrative program may be deductible for criminal penalties once the decision letter on administrative penalties takes effect to avoid duplicate execution of penalties). 2. Qi **, convicted of the crime of environmental pollution, is imprisoned 10 months and fined CNY 50,000 (The term of imprisonment shall commence upon the date judgment takes effect. If detainment has been adopted prior to the judgment, one day of administrative detention shall be offset against one day of imprisonment, i.e., the term of imprisonment starts on July 24, 2019, and terminates on May 23, 2020. The fine shall be paid within 15 days upon the date the judgment takes effect). 3. Minghe's unlawful proceeds of CNY 1,461,296.7 shall be confiscated.

Neither Minghe nor Qi ** filed an appeal; no counter-appeal was filed from the prosecution; the verdict has taken legal effect.

Legal Reasoning

The court held that China, as a party to the Vienna Convention for the Protection of the Ozone Layer and the Montreal Protocol on Substances that Deplete the Ozone Layer, should perform international obligations to protect the ozone layer. In order to fulfill the obligations, China has formulated a national ODS phase-out project and enacted policies and regulations such as the ODS Management Regulations that explicitly outlawed the use of controlled ODS. The Minutes of the Symposium on Issues Relating to the Handling of Criminal Cases of Environmental Pollution jointly issued by the Supreme People's Court, the Supreme People's Procuratorate, the Ministry of Public Security, the Ministry of Justice and the Ministry of Ecology, and the Environment clarify that controlled ODS are "other harmful substances" as defined in the crime of environmental pollution, and therefore the unlawful use of controlled ODS is a serious and punishable offense which may trigger environmental crime prosecution.

The issue of this case concerned the conviction and sentencing of the use of controlled ODS that cause environmental pollution. According to the Minutes of the Symposium on Issues Related to the Handling of Criminal Cases of Environmental Pollution, the focus must be on the concurrency of guilty act and guilty mind in handling cases of unlawful emission, dumping and disposal of other harmful substances. The actor's culpable state of mind, the severity of the polluting behavior and the toxicity of the hazardous substance must be fully assessed to determine the level of social harm caused by the offense. The Interpretation of the Supreme People's Court and the Supreme People's Procuratorate on Several Issues concerning Law Application in Handling Criminal Cases of Environmental Pollution lists situations that are defined as being "serious pollution of the environment" and "particularly serious consequences," which provides guidance for the conviction and sentencing of environmental pollution crimes. As mentioned above, the unlawful use of controlled ODS polluting can be the punishable crime of environmental pollution if the requirement is satisfied, i.e., the offense has resulted in serious pollution of the environment. According to the judicial interpretation and the Minutes of the Symposium on Issues Related to the Handling of Criminal Cases of Environmental Pollution, the focus must be on the amount of ill-gotten proceeds or the loss of public and private property, as well as the presence of other types of serious environmental pollution in handling cases of unlawful use of controlled ODS. In other words, the provisions of the judicial interpretation on the amounts of illegal gains or damages of public or private property can form the basis for the conviction and sentencing of such cases. It is noteworthy that controlled ODS, categorized as other hazardous substances, are different from radioactive wastes, wastes with infectious disease pathogens and toxic substances, and lacking scientific criteria to assess their dangerousness, toxicity, and severity of consequences.

Therefore, the court shall not base the conviction and sentencing of such cases sorely on the judicial interpretations rules concerning quantities of "illegal emission, dumping and disposal of hazardous wastes."

In this case, CFC-11, a controlled hazardous substance that causes ozone-layer depletion, is explicitly outlawed for use. Minghe, in violation of the regulations, used 849.5 tons of CFC-11 to produce insulation materials, resulting in emissions of 3049.7 kilograms, and earned illicit income of more than CNY1.46 million. The act caused serious pollution to the environment and thus constituted a crime of environmental pollution. The legal representative of Minghe, Qi **, aware that CFC-11 was banned in production still purchased the substance for the manufacture of insulation materials, causing serious environmental pollution. Qi shall be held liable for the crime of environmental pollution. Considering the amounts of controlled ODS used by Minghe and Qi **, the emissions associated with the use of CFC-11 for production and the illicit profits made from the process, the conviction, and sentencing of Minghe and Qi ** in the verdict are appropriate.

Significance

This is the first criminal case concerning environmental pollution caused by the unlawful use of controlled ODS in China and is also the first of its kind in China's rigid polyurethane (PU) foam insulation sector in a sense that the unlawful use of controlled ODS has triggered criminal sentencing. CFC-11 is a controlled and hazardous substance that causes ozone layer depletion and air pollution. As a party to the Vienna Convention for the Protection of the Ozone Layer and the Montreal Protocol on Substances that Deplete the Ozone Layer, China has committed itself to implementing international environmental treaties and issued the List of Controlled Ozone Depleting Substances on September 27, 2010, that bans the use of CFC-11 under Type I CFCs. The appropriate trial and verdict of this case showcase the "zero tolerance" approach the court system takes to crack down on the unlawful acts involving controlled ODS. The judgment can deter the rigid PU foam sector; among other relevant sectors, and the public from future offenses. This is a demonstration of the judiciary's resolution in safeguarding the global achievements of ozone layer protection and the building of a community of shared future.

Court and Members of the Collegial Bench

Court of First Instance: In Deqing Primary People's Court, Zhejiang, before Wang Kunming, Wang Jing, Wang Xuejiao

Chapter 12
Case of Zhuo * Smuggling Endangered Animals

Keywords Criminal · Smuggling of precious · rare animals · International environmental treaties · Circumstances for sentencing · Range of penalties

Basic Facts

In July 2015, Zhuo * arranged for Li ** (sentenced) to fly from the People's Republic of Bangladesh to Guangzhou Baiyun International Airport with two suitcases of turtles and took the green channel free of declaration. Li was found on the spot carrying 259 turtles which were later identified as 12 black pond turtles (Geoemydidae) and Indian roofed turtles (Pangshura tecta), both CITES Appendix I species valued at CNY 6.475 million. However, the two types of turtles smuggled in this case are not in eluded in the list of the wild animals of the Interpretation of the Supreme People's Court and the Supreme People's Procuratorate on Several Issues concerning the Application of Law in the Trial of Criminal Cases of Smuggling (hereinafter referred to as the Interpretation); it is also impossible to base the sentencing on that concerning species of same genus or family listed in the judicial interpretation.

Judgment

On October 31, 2017, the Guangzhou Intermediate People's Court handed down the criminal verdict (No. 587, [2016] First, Criminal, 01, Guangdong): "Zhuo**, guilty of smuggling precious and rare animals, is subject to 12 years imprisonment and confiscation of personal property valued at CNY 200,000." On March 19, 2018, the Guangdong High People's Court rejected Zhuo's appeal in the criminal ruling (No.

Influential Environment and Resources Cases in China (2024),
https://doi.org/10.1007/978-981-96-9562-1_12

225 [2018] Final, Criminal, Guangdong). The ruling of the Guangzhou Intermediate People's Court was affirmed.

Legal Reasoning

According to the court ruling in effect, Zhuo*, in violation of national laws and customs regulations, avoided customs duties and arranged for prohibited and endangered animals to be smuggled into China. The behavior constituted the crime of smuggling precious and rare animals, a particularly serious crime. Zhuo was the boss of the smuggling conspiracy and should be punished for organizing, participating, and masterminding the crime.

The core issues concerning the application of the law in this case are: 1. whether Zhuo *'s behavior of arranging the smuggling of CITES species yet unlisted in the List of the Interpretation constitutes the crime of smuggling precious and rare animals; 2. whether the crime is "particularly serious."

1. On whether the act constitutes the crime of smuggling precious and rare animals

Zhuo * arranged for the smuggling of live turtles which were seized on the spot and sent for appraisal. According to the appraisal result, the 247 turtles in eluded 12 black pond turtles (Geoemydidae) and Indian roofed turtles (Pangshura tecta) valued at CNY 6.475 million. Both have been listed on the CITES Appendix I effective as of June 12, 2013.

Article 151(2) of the Criminal Law of the People's Republic of China provides that Anyone who smuggles cultural relics, gold, silver, and other precious metals prohibited for export by the State or precious animals and their products prohibited for import or export by the State shall be sentenced to fixed-term imprisonment of not less than five years and not more than ten years, and shall be fined; if the circumstances are particularly serious, he shall be sentenced to fixed-term imprisonment of not less than ten years or life imprisonment, and shall have his property confiscated; if the circumstances are less serious, the penalty shall be imprisonment for a term not exceeding five years and a fine. According to Article 10 of the Interpretation, the term "rare and precious animals" as mentioned in Article 151(2) of the Criminal Law includes the wild animals under first- class or second-class state protection as included in the List of Wild Animals under Special State Protection, the wild animals in Appendices I and II to the Convention on International Trade in Endangered Species of Wild Fauna and Flora, and the domesticated and bred ones of the aforesaid animals. As China is a party to CITES, the terrestrial animal species listed in Appendix I and II of CITES that are not endemic to China have been included into first-class or second-class state protection respectively. Despite the fact that the black pond turtle and the Indian roofed turtle in question are not endemic to China and are in the same taxonomic order but different families and genera with Horsfield's tortoise (Testudo horsfieldii) and impressed tortoise (Manouria impressa) listed in the Appendix to the

Interpretation, both are precious and rare animals listed on CITES Appendix I and protected by the Criminal Law of the People's Republic of China.

The court held that Zhuo * violated national laws and regulations and evaded customs duties by arranging for prohibited animals, i.e.,12 live black pond turtles and 247 live Indian roofed turtles, to be smuggled into the country. The behavior constituted the crime of smuggling precious and rare animals.

2. On whether Zhuo's smuggling of precious and rare animals fits the "particularly serious circumstances"

Article 151(2) of the Criminal Law of the People's Republic of China provides for three categories of punishment for the crime of smuggling precious and rare animals: less serious, general, and particularly serious. Article 9(3) of the Interpretation stipulates those circumstances where the quantity of smuggled animals under first-class or second-class state protection reaches the quantitative criteria set out in Appendix (1) to this Interpretation may be deemed "particularly serious." According to Article 10(2) of the Interpretation, the smuggling of rare and precious animals not mentioned in the Appendix to this Interpretation shall be punished by reference to the quantitative criteria set out in the Appendix for animals of the same genus or family. The Appendix to the Interpretation provides no quantitative circumstances for black pond turtle and the Indian roofed turtle in question, nor for animals of the same genus or family.

However, according to the quantity-based range of penalties concerning two types of tortoise endemic to China, i.e., Russian tortoise and the impressed tortoise (both belonging to the genus Tortoise): Smuggling less than four Horsfield's tortoises is a "less serious circumstance"; smuggling four to seven is a circumstance subject to "an imprisonment of five to ten years plus a fine"; smuggling eight or more constitutes a "particularly serious circumstance"; smuggling less than six impressed tortoise is a "Less serious circumstance"; six to nine is a circumstance subject to an imprisonment of five to ten years plus a fine smuggling 10 or more is a "particularly serious circumstance":

In summary, the black pond turtle and the Indian roofed turtle, though not endemic to China, are in the same taxonomic order but different families and genera with Horsfield's tortoise and impressed tortoise listed on the Appendix to the Interpretation of the Supreme People's Court and the Supreme People's Procuratorate on Several Issues concerning the Application of Law in the Trial of Criminal Cases of Smuggling. No species share the same family or genus with the two types of tortoises. the objects of the crime in this case. In this context, the principle of legality and punishment shall apply in the handling cases of smuggling of species protected by the CITES Appendices. If the sentencing cannot be based on that of species of the same genus or family, the quantitative sentencing standard for smuggling species of the same order, the same class, or the same family shall apply class by class to determine the seriousness of the crime and the range of penalties; the rulings should be based on the quantities of the smuggled and the value to ensure punishment fits the crime.

In this case, Zhuo * arranged for 259 black pond turtles and Indian roofed turtles, non-native species valued at CNY 6,475,000, to be smuggled into China, which are 32 and 25 times respectively the standards for sentencing the "particularly serious smuggling" of Horsfield's tortoises and impressed tortoises in circumstances. The crime involved large amounts of money; producing much more social harm than that of smuggling 8 or more Horsfield*s tortoise or 10 or more impressed tortoises. Therefore, under the quantitative standards for sentencing the smuggling of Horsfield's tortoises and impressed tortoises, Zhuo's act should be deemed as a "particularly serious circumstance" as stipulated in Article 151(2) of the Criminal Law of the People's Republic of China.

Significance

This is a case of smuggling of precious and rare animals listed on the appendix of the Convention on International Trade in Endangered Species of Wild Fauna and Flora. Biodiversity is essential to human survival and development, and wildlife species are an integral comp orient of biodiversity: No trade, no killing. Protecting wildlife is the responsibility of us all. As a Party to CITES, China performs its obligations under the Convention to fight the unlawful and criminal acts of smuggling endangered species. In this case, Zhuo * violated national laws and customs regulations and evaded customs duties by having the prohibited and endangered animals unlawfully brought into China. The People's Court found the crime particularly serious and imposed a sentence in accordance with the law, demonstrating the People's Courts determination to crack down on crimes against wildlife resources. The trial and verdict of this case have sent a strong deterrent message and awakened the public awareness of respecting law and protecting the ecosystem, especially the wildlife species within.

Courts and Members of the Collegial Bench

Court of First Instance: In Guangzhou Intermediate People's Court, Guangdong, before Xing Fu, Jiang Jinquan, Xu Yuanyuan

Court of Second Instance: In Guangdong High People's Court, before Wu Tiecheng, Deng Minbo, Shi Chunyan

Chapter 13
Case of Zhang ** et al. Intentionally Damaging the Python Peak

Keywords Criminal · Intentional destruction of historic · scenic sites · World Geological Sites · Climbing with spikes · Serious damage · Expert opinion

Basic Facts

In April 2017, Zhang **, Mao **, and Zhang * planned a mountaineering trip on WeChat and decided to climb the "Python" rock pillar (also known as the Python Peak) in the Sanqing Mountain Scenic Site. Zhang **, Mao **, and Zhang * arrived at the bottom of Python Peak with electric drills, pitons (i.e., expansion bolts, made of stainless steel), hammers, ropes, among other tools around 4:00 a.m. on April 15, 2017. Zhang ** climbed first with Mao ** and Zhang * towing the rope beneath for protection. Zhang ** hit pitons into the rock into the mountain side Fong the way; he drilled holes on the rock with the electric drill, hit the pitons into the holes with the hammer, tightened them with a wrench, and fixed the rope around the spikes. In this way; Zhang ** reached the top around 6:49 a.m., followed by Mao ** who had been towing the rope for protection and reached the top around 7:00 a.m. assisted by the rope fixated by Zhang earlier. At the top of Python Peak, Zhang gave the remaining tools to Mao who then descended with the rope and took them back to the hotel. Later he returned to Python Peak and caught by the staff of Sanqing Mountain Administration Committee and taken to the local police station. When the two males went climbing, Zhang * the female, towed the rope beneath for protection. She later fetched a drone from the hotel. Assisted by the rope fixated by Zhang **, Zhang * reached the top of the Python Peak around 7:30 a.m. and used the drone to film. Persuaded by the staff, Zhang *and Zhang **got to the bottom of the Python Peak around 9:00 a.m. and were taken to the police station. The site investigation revealed that Zhang ** hammered 26 pitons into the Python Peak. According to the expert

Influential Environment and Resources Cases in China (2024),
https://doi.org/10.1007/978-981-96-9562-1_13

evidence, the trio's behavior has caused serious damage to the Python Peak, a World Geological Site.

Judgment

The Intermediate People's Court of Shangrao City Jiangxi Province, made a criminal verdict on December 26, 2019 (No.34 [2018] First, Criminal, 11, Jiangxi): "1. Zhang **, convicted of the crime of intentionally destroying places with historic interest and scenic beauty; imprisoned one year and fined CNY 100,000; 2. Mao **, convicted of the crime of intentionally destroying places with historic interest and scenic beauty is imprisoned six months, suspended for one year; and fined CNY 50,000; 3. Zhang *, convicted of the crime of intentionally destroying places with historic interest and scenic beauty, is exempted from criminal punishment; 4. The four cell phones, one drone, two walkie-talkies, ropes, hammers, electric drills, and pitons involved in the case shall be confiscated." Zhang ** filed an appeal after the verdict was announced. On May 18, 2020, the Jiangxi High People's Court issued a ruling (No. 44 [2020] Final, Criminal, Jiangxi), to affirm the original sentence.

Legal Reasoning

According to the court ruling, the points of contention in this case included:

(a) Admissibility of the evidence

China is lacking judicial appraisal institutions competent to assess the degree of damage caused by hammering 26 pitons into the rock. However, whether the climbers' behavior constituted a crime depended on the degree of such a damage. Under Article 87[1] of the Interpretation of the Supreme People's Court on the Application of the "Criminal Procedure Law of the People's Republic of China," the court may appoint and hire those with expertise to verify matters outside the experience of accredited judicial appraisal institutions or beyond the scope of law and judicial interpretations and consult the verification report for conviction and sentencing. The relevant provisions of this section shall apply with reference to the examination and determination of the verification report. Where the verifier refuses to testify in court after being notified by the court, the verification report shall not be used for conviction and sentencing. Therefore, it was reasonable to hire people with specialist knowledge to verify whether the act of driving 26 pitons into the rock caused serious damage to the Python Peak. All the four experts in this case with years of experience in the field of geology research published a large myriad of papers or theses

[1] Article 100, "Interpretation by the Supreme People's Court Regarding the Application of the Criminal Procedure Law of the People's Republic of China" (2021).

or led major research projects in geology, i.e., they were fully qualified to evaluate the degree of damage to the Python Peak, a specialized geological matter. The four experts fit the definition of "those with expertise." In the expert opinions co-signed by the four and commissioned by the investigative authorities, the experts discussed, analyzed, and reached a clear conclusion on how much damage the pitons caused to the Python Peak based on their specialist knowledge, on-site investigation, and evidence examination. Upon the notification of the court, two of them appeared in court as examiners to elaborate on the formation of the expert opinions and took questions from both sides and the judges. The expert conclusion, being clear and in line with the procedural rules, was considered admissible. In summary, the expert opinion in this case conformed the legal requirements on the expert qualification and the procedure. Submitted as evidence, the expert opinion fully complied with Article 197 under the Criminal Procedure Law of the People's Republic of China, as well as Article 87 under the Interpretation of the Supreme People's Court on the Application of the Criminal Procedure Law of the People's Republic of China Regarding the Issuance of Examination Reports by Specialists, and thus should serve as a basis for conviction and sentencing.

(b) Fact-finding about the damage

Sanqing Mountain was listed by the State Council in 1988 as a National Key Scenic Spot and then became a UNESCO World Natural Heritage Site in 2008 and a World Geopark in 2012. As the iconic landscape of Sanqing Mountain, the Python Peak is unique and precious, not only as a non-renewable and rare natural resource asset, but also as a common property with great scientific, aesthetic, and economic value that can be of sustainable use by all mankind. The Python Peak is a giant granite formation produced by long- lasting weathering and disintegration. It is a 128-metre-high rock pillar with a diameter of only 7 meters at its thinnest point. In this case, the four experts hired by the investigating authorities submitted their expert opinions on the rock pillar's value, cause of formation, structure, and the damage caused by the trio's behavior via on-site investigation, evidence examination, and science-based analysis. The four experts, from a geological specialists perspective, concluded that the rock climbers' behavior caused permanent damage to the core landscape of the World Natural Heritage, the Python Peak, destroying the basic attributes of natural heritage, i.e., its naturalness, primitive ness, and integrity. The defendants drove at least four pitons into the section already in a fragile state, further weakening and destabilizing the rock pillar. The 26 pitons made the pillar more susceptible to physical, chemical, and biological weathering, created crevices in the rock, increased the rate of erosion, and might even led to disintegration. According to Article 4.2.1 of the Interpretation of the Supreme People's Court and the Supreme People's Procuratorate on Several Issues concerning the Application of Law in Handling Criminal Cases of Obstruction of Cultural Relics Management and the expert opinions, the court concluded that the behavior of Zhang **, Mao **, and Zhang * in violation of Article 324 of the Criminal Law of the People's Republic of China by causing "serious damage" to the scenic spot, were found guilty of the crime of damaging scenic and historic sites.

The core areas in the scenic spots are protected by China's criminal law. The Sanqing Mountain Scenic Spot has been inscribed as one of the natural properties on UNESCO's World Heritage List and a World Geopark. The Python Peak Geological Site, a precious iconic landscape at the core of the scenic spot, is a non-renewable natural resource asset that can be of sustainable use with its significant scientific, aesthetic, and economic value. The trio, in violation of the social administrative order; scaled the Python Peak in a destructive manner, i.e., drilling 26 pitons into the granite pillar, which caused serious damage to the Python Peak. The circumstance was particularly serious; the behavior constituted the crime of intentional destruction of scenic and historical relics and was thus punishable. The conviction of the rock climbers is not only a negative assessment of the acts they have committed, but also warns the public against any misconduct against resources and the environment. It has awakened the public awareness of ecological civilization and encouraged them to take care of natural resources and the environment that provide the foundation for humanity's survival and development. The sentence imposed by the Court of First Instance was not in appropriate based on the status and role of Zhang **, Mao **, and Zhang * in the joint crime and the circumstances. The appeal for acquittal filed by Zhang ** and his attorney was rejected. The first trial verdict was based on the corroborated facts of the crime committed by Zhang **, Mao **, and Zhang *. The evidence was sufficient, the conviction was accurate, the sentences were appropriate, and the trial procedure was lawful.

Significance

This is China's first criminal case concerning intentional destruction of scenic spots. Sanqing Mountain is a World Natural Heritage Site, a World Geological Park, and a National 5-A Scenic Spot. The Python Peak is the landmarks and core scenic area in Sanqing Mountain. The rock climbers in this case scaled the Python Peak using destructive methods. By drilling 26 pitons into the granite pillar, they caused serious damage to the rock. Considering the features of the geological relics and the extent of the damage, the People's Court found the act in question "serious" and constituted the crime of intentional destruction of a national protected relic. Since no accredited judicial appraisal agencies is capable of assessing the extent of damage the scenic spot is suffering, it was reasonable for the People's Court to base the conviction and sentencing on expert opinion issued by those with specialist knowledge. By punishing the crime of intentional destruction of monuments and sites, this case not only highlights the urgency of the protection of monuments and sites, but also awakens the public awareness on ecological civilization and encourages them to care natural resources and the environment which are essential to the survival and development of human beings.

Courts and Members of the Collegial Bench

Court of First Instance: In Shangrao Intermediate People's Court, Jiangxi, before Zheng Xianghua, Cheng Xiaobin, Zhou Yan, Xu Risheng, Ma Liping, Chen Lifang, Wang Yuzhen

Court of Second Instance: In Jiangxi High People's Court, before Hu Shuzhu, Huang Xunrong, Wang Huijun

Chapter 14
Civil Public Interest Litigation Case: People's Procuratorate of Shangrao, Jiangxi v. Zhang ** et al., for Causing Ecological Damage to the Python Peak

Keywords Civil · Civil public interest litigation of ecological damage · Amount of damages · Conditional value method · Imputation principle

Basic Facts

Shangrao People's Procuratorate filed a public interest case, claiming that Zhang **, Mao **, and Zhang * climbed the Python Peak in a destructive manner and drove 26 pitons into the Python Peak, the core scenic area of Sanqing Mountain, a World Natural Heritage Site, and a World Geological Park. The act caused serious damage to the rock pillar and infringed on the interest and rights of the public. Therefore, the trio was required to pay damages of CNY 11.9 million in minimum, jointly, and severally; for damaging the non-use value of the Python Peak, extend public apology in the nationally renowned media; and jointly and severally pay CNY 150,000 to compensate for the expert fee previously paid by the prosecutors. In response to the prosecution request, the defense argued that this case was not environmental public interest litigation, rendering the prosecution in eligible to bring civil public interest litigation. The trio claimed that the act was not performed with a guilty mind, nor did they cause serious damage to the Python Peak. As risk of injury did not equal injury, they behavior constituted no infringement; the "Assessment Report for the Damage of Python Peak of Sanqing Mountain" (hereinafter referred to as the "assessment report") issued by the three experts was inadmissible.

According to the court's findings, Zhang **, Mao **, and Zhang * arrived at the bottom of Python Peak with electric drills, pitons (i.e., expansion bolts made of stain less steel), hammers, ropes, among other tools around 4:00 a.m. on April 15, 2017. Zhang ** climbed first with Mao ** and Zhang * towing the rope beneath for protection. Zhang ** hit pitons into the rock into the mountainside along the way; he drilled holes on the rock with the electric drill, hit the pitons into the holes with the

Influential Environment and Resources Cases in China (2024),
https://doi.org/10.1007/978-981-96-9562-1_14

hammer, tightened them with a wrench, and fixed the rope around the spikes. In this way, Zhang ** reached the top with Mao ** in company towing the rope for safety. Mao also reached the top assisted by the rope previously fixated by Zhang. Following Zhang **'s route, the female climber, Zhang * reached the top of the Python Peak later and used the drone to film. Caught by the staff working at the site, the three were taken to the police station. The site investigation revealed that Zhang ** hammered 26 pitons into the Python Peak. As assessed by experts, the assessed lost value in this case should be no lower than the minimum loss of the non-use value of the Python Peak incurred by this incident, which was CNY 11.9 million.

Judgment

The Shangrao Intermediate People's Court handed down the civil judgment (No. 303, [2018] First, Civil, 11, Jiangxi) on December 27, 2019: "Zhang **, Zhang * and Mao ** shall extend a public apology on a national media within 10 days after the judgment takes effect and the content of the apology shall be determined by the Shangrao Intermediate People's Court; the three shall jointly and severally pay CNY six million in damages for losses of environmental resources. The payment shall be made to an account designated by the Shangrao Intermediate People's Court within 30 days after the judgment comes into effect, and the sum will be used for ecological protection and restoration; the three shall also pay CNY 150,000 to compensate for the expert fee previously paid by the prosecutors within 10 days after the judgment comes into effect". Zhang ** and Zhang * appealed against the ruling. The Jiangxi High People's Court made a verdict on May 18, 2020, ([2020] Gan Civil Verdict Final No. 317), rejecting the appeal and affirming the decision of the lower court.

Legal Reasoning

The court held that the python peak, a world renowned geological heritage site, was a unique, precious, and non-renewable natural resource asset as well as a common property with great scientific, aesthetic, and economic value that should be shared by both present and future generations. In this case, the defendants took a destructive climbing method, causing damage to the Python Peak. The behavior was beyond the reasonable use of natural resources and infringed on the environmental rights and interests of an unspecified large group of people. The interest of an unspecified majority of people, is the definition of the public interest. Regarding the damaging consequences, the experts concluded that the behavior caused serious damage to the naturalness, primitiveness, and integrity of the Python Peak, making it more susceptible to physical, chemical, and biological weathering. The defendants drove four pitons into the thinnest and most fragile section of the granite pillar; further weakening the rock. The first consequence in the expert opinion described a "done" state, i.e., the damage to the naturalness, originality, and integrity of the Python Peak perceivable to ordinary people. The second and third consequences in the expert opinion described a real and perilous state. The pitons driven by Zhang ** et al. increased the likelihood of injury, i.e., probability of the hazard occurring. This increase in the probability was "done" and the risk of damage Python Peak actually increased, which constituted substantial injury. Therefore, the risk of "aggravation," and "even disintegration" of the Python described in the expert opinion based on the scientific and specialist knowledge, constituted a significant risk of harm to the public interest.

On quantifying the injury caused by Zhang **, Mao **, and Zhang * to the Python Peak, no appointed judicial appraisal institution in China is competent to provide appraisal service. Shangrao City People's Procuratorate therefore commissioned a group of experts from Jiangxi University of Finance and Economics to assess the losses incurred to the Python Peak and produce the "Assessment Report" using the conditional valuation approach. The Assessment Report concluded that "the assessed lost value of the Python Peak should not be lower than the minimum losses of the rock's non-use value caused by the incident, which should be CNY 11.9 million." As an internationally accepted approach, conditional valuation approach is among the recommendations from the Ministry of Ecology and Environment, for it is science-based and particularly suitable to assess ecosystem services such as unique landscapes and cultural relics of which option value accounts for a greater proportion. However, conditional valuation focuses on "preferences," i.e., conducting preference surveys on environmental matters via questionnaires, votes, and inquiries. The results could be subjective, random, and full of uncertainties.

Therefore, the Assessment Report was science-based but lacked certainties. In the absence of a more suitable way to measure the damage, according to Article 23 of the Interpretation of the Supreme People's Court on Several Issues concerning the Application of Law to the Trial of Environmental Civil Public Interest Litigation, "where the cost of ecological restoration is difficult to determine or the specific amount required for identification is obviously too high, the people's court may base the decision on the scope and extent of pollution and ecological damage, the scarcity of the environment, and the extent of the damage, the scarcity of the ecological environment, the difficulty of restoring the ecosystem, the operating costs of pollution prevention and control equipment, the benefits gained by the defendant(s) as a result of the infringement and the degree of seriousness and may consult the competent authorities in charge of supervision and management of environmental resources protection and experts." The court, having had considered the scientific nature and uncertainties of the conditional valuation approach adopted in the assessment report, as well as the legal, social, and economic factors of the case, the claims of the plaintiff in the first instance, the corroborated facts, the parties' ability to perform court orders and the economic status of Jiangxi, etc., made a reasonable decision on the damages valuated by assessment report, and made a discretionary determination that the loss was worth CNY 6 million.

Zhang **, Mao **, and Zhang * were veteran rock climbers, fully aware of the unique value of the Python Peak, an iconic landscape located in the Sanqing Mountain Scenic Site. On driving 26 pitons into the rock pillar, the trio did not consult experts beforehand nor did they stay clear of the fragile section during the process, which resulted in damage to the whole rock from top to bottom. The trio have intentionally or recklessly caused damage to the Python Peak and thus should be found guilty and liable of the tort. The defendants scaled a world geological and natural site, the Python Peak, using destructive pitons, resulting in irreparable and permanent damage to the public interest. Their behavior constituted joint infringement. Protecting the environment is a shared responsibility among all peoples and can only be achieved with the most robust system and the strictest rule of law. The verdict that held the trio jointly liability for environmental tort not only raises the public awareness of ecological civilization but also addresses people's growing need for a beautiful environment. It also calls on the world to fight for global ecological civilization, and to protect the environment on which human beings depend for survival and development.

Significance

The case is a civil public interest litigation for ecological damage arising from the deliberate destruction of a famous monument. Sanqing Mountain is a World Natural Heritage Site, a World Geological Park and a National 5-A Scenic Spot. It is unique and precious not only as a non-renewable and rare natural resource asset, but also as a common property with great scientific, aesthetic and economic value that can be of sustainable use by all mankind. The Python Peak is the iconic and core scenic area in Sanqing Mountain. The rock climbers in this case scaled the Python Peak using destructive methods. By drilling 26 pitons into the granite pillar; they caused serious damage to the rock. The People's Court punished the perpetrators for committing the crime of intention ally destroying famous and historical sites and deterred the public from any misconduct against state-protected famous and historical sites. The court heard the civil public interest litigation for ecological damage and ordered the defendants to restore the ecosystem after considering the nature of the case and the expert opinions. The judgment is significant as it awakens the public awareness of ecological civilization to protect the environment essential to the survival and development of human beings. Together with the previous criminal case, it showcases China's commitment to provide all-dimensional protection of the environment. The alignment between criminal liability with civil liability has demonstrated the punitive function of criminal law and the restorative function of public interest litigation.

Courts and Members of the Collegial Bench

Court of First Instance: In Shangrao Intermediate People's Court, before Zheng Xianghua, Cheng Xiaobin, Zhou Yan, Xu Risheng, Ma Liping, Chen Lifang, Wang Yuzhen

Court of Second Instance: In Jiangxi High People's Court, before Hu Shuzhu, Huang Xunrong, Wang Huijun

Chapter 15 Civil Public Interest Litigation Case of Ecological Damage: People's Procuratorate of Taizhou City, Jiangsu Province v. Wang ** et 59 for Illegal Fishing of Elvers

Keywords Civil · Civil public interest litigation for ecological damage · Illegal fishing · Joint infringement · Compensation for ecological damage

Basic Facts

Yangtze elvers are economically important fish species prohibited from harvest. In the first half of 2018,38 people, including Dong ** were in the business of unlawful fishing of elvers using prohibited gears in the trunk stream of Yangtze River and profited from selling the catch. Wang ** and 12 others, knowing that the Yangtze eel fries were unlawfully harvested, still formed a partnership to acquire the elvers individually or jointly and sell them for profit. The partnership acquired a total of 116,999 elvers from a seven-person group, in eluding Gao **, and a 38-person group, including Dong **, all engaged in unlawful trading or fishing activities. Qin ** bought 40,263 elvers from Wang ** and others on several occasions, knowing that the elvers were illegally harvested.

Wang ** and others were found guilty of illegally catching aquatic products and concealing the criminal proceeds in a separate criminal verdict in force. On July 15, 2019, the People's Procuratorate of Taizhou, Jiangsu, brought civil public interest litigation against Wang ** and 59 others for damaging the ecological resources of the Yangtze River and harming the public interests by illegally fishing, selling, and acquiring Yangtze elvers.

Influential Environment and Resources Cases in China (2024),
https://doi.org/10.1007/978-981-96-9562-1_15

Judgment

The Nanjing Intermediate People's Court handed down civil judgment (No. 2005, [2019] First, Civil, 01, Jiangsu) on October 24, 2019: 1. Wang ** and 12 other illegal acquirers shall jointly and severally compensate for the loss of ecological resources caused by the illegal trading of elvers for more than CNY 8.58 million; 2. other buyers and fishermen are liable for compensation, either depending on the quantity of elvers in the illegal trading or fishing activities they were part of, or jointly and severally with the lead purchasers. The Jiangsu High People's Court rejected the appeal filed by 11 defendants including Wang and affirmed the original judgment in the civil judgment (No. 1734, [2019] Final, Civil, Jiangsu) on December 31, 2019.

Legal Reasoning

According to the court ruling in force:

(a) When illegal fishing that causes serious damage to ecological resources takes place for the sole purpose of selling and when those in the business of illegal fishing and acquiring have formed a buyer–supplier relationship, the act of acquisition can be deemed as a trigger of illegal fishing and a contributing factor to ecological damage. Therefore, the acquirers should be held jointly and severally liable with the fishmen for causing loss and damage to ecological resources.

Eel elver, listed as "Endangered" on the IUCN Red List in 2014, is also included in the list of key protected fish species in Jiangsu. Eel elvers with distinctive characteristics are not for direct consumption. Fishing for this species is not economically viable if not for the purposes of large-scale acquisition. Unlawful fishing, only profitable with acquisition, is impossible to take place continuously and repeatedly. The robust demand drives illegal fishing and acquisition. The act of acquisition in this case was routinized and highly organized, with each participant having a clear understanding of their roles in the chain of interests and the purpose of making profit through illegal fishing, sale and acquisition, sale at inflated prices, and farming for sale, etc. The fishermen used nets with mesh smaller than permitted to catch baby eels: the buyers were fully aware of the physical features of the catch, i.e., they knew that fishing for species of such a small size would entail methods different from those used for other fish. The outlaw fishermen used "fine mesh nets" to catch elvers in large quantities and did that multiple times in the trunk stream of the Yangtze River during the fish breeding season when fishing was clearly banned. The large-scale and repeated fishing of elvers in the trunk stream of Yangtze River, especially during fishery closure, may inevitably cause losses to ecological resources and the destruction of biodiversity in the Yangtze River. There was a deliberate intent on the part of the buyers and fishermen to allow damage to the eel stock and other ecological resources to occur. A buyer-supplier relationship was created and a complete chain of interests was thus formed in which neighboring links are highly coordinated to benefit from illegal fishing, establishing the causal link between the actors' behavior and the subsequent harm to the Yangtze River ecosystem.

The chain of interests should be completely cut off at the source to prevent illegal fishing so that joint infringers who illegally acquire and sell eel elvers are required to pay the monetary price and held jointly and severally liable with outlaw fishermen for the damage to the Yangtze River ecosystem within the scope of the ecological resource damage they are involved in.

(b) Where it is impossible to calculate the loss of ecological resources, the court shall take into account the scope and extent of ecological damage, the scarcity of resources involved and other factors to assess the destructiveness, the time sensitivity and location specificality surrounding the alleged unlawful practice and make judgments as appropriate based on expert opinions.

The illegal fishing was carried out using nets made of very fine mesh. The sensitivity of the fishing time, the high frequency of the fishing activity, and the specificity of the fishing location all posed a serious threat to the elver stock and affected other fish species in the Yangtze River, putting biodiversity of the Yangtze River ecosystem and the ecological resources in this area at great risk. Under Article 23 of the Interpretation of the Supreme People's Court on Several Issues concerning the Application of Law to the Trial of Environmental Civil Public Interest Litigation Cases and considering the actual damage to ecological resources caused by the illegal fishing of eel elvers, the court determined that the loss of ecological resources was 2.5 times the value of the loss of eel stock based on two main points:

1. The destructive nature of the fishing method—the fishmen used prohibited gears, i.e., nets with mesh smaller than what is permitted by the Notice of the Ministry of Agriculture on the Minimum Mesh Size Permitted for Fishing and Transitional Fishing Gears in the Think Stream of the Yangtze River, which is no less than 3 mm. The gears would inevitably trap by-catch, including other small fish, and seriously damage the aquatic resources in the area. The quantity of eel elvers involved in the case, 116,999, indicated that the illegal fishing activity must have occurred many times in a large area using many gears, which definitely caused great harm to the ecological resources of the Yangtze River.
2. The sensitivity of the time and the place wherein the offense occurred—the fishing and acquisition activities in question primarily occur during the closed fishing season, which is a crucial spawning time for the aquatic resources of the Yangtze River, including eel stock. The offenses occurred in the main stream of the Yangtze River, the migratory route of the Japanese eels. The young eels leaving their natural range were fished for on the migratory route and sold for profit, which not only hindered the eels' reproductive success but also trapped other aquatic species. This could cause fish stocks and their foods to dwindle, thus leading to the destruction of adjacent links in the food chain and the damage of biodiversity in the Yangtze River.

The court also clarified in the ruling that, to balance the need to protect ecological resources and the defendant's right to subsistence, the return of illegal proceeds could be deducted from the ecological damages payment. Also, considering the defendants' inability to pay the damages in full, part of the compensation can be paid by service, such as participating in activities that protect the ecosystem for the Yangtze River or other activities for public interest or assisting the governance of the riverbank along the Yangtze River, in eluding rein force merit, clean-up, and so on.

Significance

This case is the first of its kind in China in which those engaged in purchasing, sales, and fishing of eel elvers in the Yangtze River were jointly and severally held liable for ecological damage. By holding each perpetrator involved responsible for ecological restoration in accordance with the law, the illegal chain of interests was cut off at source, and the rule of adjudication governing the "whole chain" was established. It showcases the determination and strength of the People's Court to protect the ecosystem of the Yangtze River with the most robust system and the most stringent rule of law. The court also relied on expert opinions to measure the consequences of ecological damage, calculated the loss of ecological resources, and allowed for the payment of compensation for ecological damage in the form of service, providing an effective option for ecological restoration. The judgment is of great significance in maintaining ecological security in the Yangtze River region, strengthening the protection of aquatic biodiversity in the Yangtze River, and forming a green development pattern of harmonious co-existence between man and nature.

Courts and Members of the Collegial Bench

Court of First Instance: Nanjing Intermediate People's Court, Jiangsu, before Chen Ying, Jiang Li, Liu Shanglei, Liu Boxiang, Lu Yaling, Zhu Jing, Hu Chun sen

Court of Second Instance: Jiangsu High People's Court, before Liu Jiangong, Zhao Li, Zang Jing

Chapter 16
Civil Preventative Public Interest Litigation Case of Peacock Conservation: Friends of Nature Environmental Research Institute of Chaoyang District, Beijing v. Hydrochina Corporation Xinping Development Co., Ltd

Keywords Civil · Civil environmental public interest litigation · Damage to social · public interests · Major risks · Endangered Species of Wild Fauna · Flora

Basic Facts

The Jiasa River Class I Hydro power Station Project was developed and constructed by Hydrochina Corporation Xinping Development Co., Ltd. (hereinafter referred to as "Xinping Company"). Powerchina Kunming Engineering Corporation Limited (hereinafter referred to as "Kunming Engineering Corporation") was the general contractor of the project and the technical entity commissioned to prepare the Environmental Impact Assessment Report for the Project (hereinafter referred to as the "EIA Report"). Located in Xinping County, Yunnan province (southwest China), the project was about 6.5 kilometers upstream from Shuitang Town of Xinping County and was developed in the form of a concrete-face rockfill dam (maximum height: 175.5 meters, normal reservoir water level: 675 meters). The flooded areas of the dam included the riverbasins of Jiasa River, Shiyang River and its tributaries Lvzhi River and Xiaojiang River, all located in the upper reaches of the Red River, affecting eight towns in Xinping County and Shuangbai County. From 2011 to 2015, the Project received official replies and approvals in terms of land use, EIA, and construction permit, among others, from the National Development and Reform Commission, the former Ministry of Land and Resources, the Ministry of Ecology and Environment, and other relevant authorities. On July 21, 2017, the General Office of the Ministry of Ecology and Environment issued a Letter on Post-Environmental Impact Assessment of the Jiasa River Class I Hydro power Station on the Main Stream of the Red (Yuan) River in Yunnan Province (hereinafter referred to as the "Post-EIA Letter") to Xinping Company, ordering the company to conduct a post- environmental impact assessment, adopt possible measures to mitigate the potential risk, and

Influential Environment and Resources Cases in China (2024),
https://doi.org/10.1007/978-981-96-9562-1_16

file the measures with the Ministry of Ecology and Environment. The letter further requested that before completion of the post-environmental impact assessment, no water should be stored for power generation. Xinping Company then suspended the construction of the project altogether since August 2017 till now. By the time the construction suspended, the preparation works of the Project had been completed and the diversion tunnels had been built.

The construction of the project may affect green peafowls, which are typical tropical and subtropical forest birds mostly found in evergreen broadleaved forests, deciduous forests, and mixed forests in river valleys. They are omnivorous and rare species evaluated as national Class I protected animal and are listed as endangered species in China's Red List of Endangered Species.

For issues concerning green peafowls, the Intermediate People's Court of Kunming City, the court of first instance of the case, delivered a letter to the Forestry and Grassland Bureau of Yunnan Province, and the Forestry and Grassland Bureau of Yunnan Province replied on April 4, 2019. The Intermediate People's Court of Kunming City then requested the Bureau to share access to the Report on the Survey of the Status of Green Peacock Population in the Middle and Upper Reaches of Yuan River it compiled. The report stated that upon completion of the Jiasa River Class I Hydropower Station, the water stored in the reservoir would flood valley areas below 680 meters above sea level and have a relatively great impact on the current suitable habitats for green peafowls, including their sand bathing grounds, riverbank courtship grounds, and others. In addition, the renovation and rebuilding of the roads in the flooded areas as a result of the construction of the Hydropower Station would also cause damage to the habitats for wild animals such as green peafowls; and that the impact of the suspension of the Project should also be assessed, and measures should be taken to protect and restore the habitats for green peafowl, among others. On June 29, 2018, the People's Government of Yunnan Province issued the Notice on Releasing Ecological Redlines in Yunnan Province, announcing the protected areas within the ecological redline of Yunnan Province. According to the Annex 1 of the document, the Distribution Map of Redline zones of Ecological Protection in Yunnan Province, most of the flooded areas of the Jiasa River Class I Hydropower Station was within the scope of the redline zone for water and soil conservation as part of the dry-hot valleys, hills, and plains along the Red (Yuan) River, in which green peafowls were identified as one of the key protected species.

Another species affected was Cycas chenii, a national Class I protected plant, in eluded in the Red List of Biological Species in Yunnan Province (2017 Edition) as a critically endangered species after 2015. In its argument, the plaintiff Friends of Nature Environmental Research Institute of Chaoyang District Beijing Municipality (hereinafter referred to as the "Friends of Nature") submitted photos of Cycas chenii it took in the valley of Lvzhi River, Shiyang River, and other flooded areas of the Jiasa River Class I Hydropower Station. Witness Liu * (assistant researcher of the Chinese Academy of Sciences) testified before court that Cycas chenii was distributed only in the Red River Basin of China across the world. According to International Union for Conservation of Nature (IUCN), Cycas chenii should be classified as an endangered species (EN). Friends of Nature sued in the Intermediate People's Court of Kunming City, requesting the people's court to order that Xinping Company and Kunming Design Institute should jointly eliminate the risk of damage to green peafowls, Cycas chenii, and other rare and endangered wild animals and plants, tropical monsoon forests, and tropical rain forests presented by the construction of the Jiasa River Class I Hydropower Station. The construction of the hydropower station should be immediately suspended, and no water should be impounded into the hydropower station, and no vegetation should be cut within the flooded area of the station.

Judgment

On March 16, 2020, the Intermediate People's Court of Kunming City; Yunnan Province issued the Civil Judgment (No. 2299 [2017] First, Civil, 01, Yunnan):

1. Xinping Company should immediately suspend the construction of the Jiasa River Class I Hydropower Station based on the existing environmental impact assessment result, and should neither impound water nor cut any vegetation in the flooded areas of the hydropower station. Follow-up actions for the hydropower station should be decided by the competent administrative authorities depending on the post-EIA results of the project, together with the mitigation plan by Xinping Company submitted to the Ministry of Ecology and Environment as requested;
2. Xinping Company should pay Friends of Nature CNY 80,000 for reasonable expenses incurred by the lawsuit within 30 days after this judgment took effect;
3. All other claims of Friends of Nature should be dismissed.

Following the judgment, Friends of Nature, on the grounds that the construction of the Jiasa River Class I Hydropower Station should be permanently canceled, appealed the decision. Xinping Company; on the other hand, held that as the construction of the hydropower station had been suspended and already fell within the ecological redline, the claims of Friends of Nature should be dismissed altogether, also appealed. The High People's Court of Yunnan Province rendered the Civil Judgment (No. 824 [2020] Final, Civil, Yunnan) on December 22, 2020, dismissing the appeals, affirming the original judgment.

Legal Reasoning

The court's effective judgment held the following: This case fell under the statutory circumstance that "presents major risk of damaging the public interest" as set forth in Article 1 of the Interpretation of the Supreme People's Court on Several Issues concerning the Application of Law in the Trial of Environmental Civil Public Interest Action Cases, providing that "...files a lawsuit against any activity that pollutes the environment and damages the ecology, which has damaged the public interest or presents major risk of damaging the public interest." This case was a preventive environmental public interest action. Preventive environmental public interest actions go beyond the traditional judicial thinking where litigation is used as a way of remedy -no remedy until there is damage. However, in environmental cases, as prescribed by China's Environmental Protection Law, the principle of "protection and prevention first" should be followed. Preventive environmental public interest litigation is a perfect illustration of the principle in judicial practice. The essential element for preventive environmental public interest litigation to proceed is to prove the existence of material risk of damage to the environment caused by a series of acts. In this case. Friends of Nature presented evidence that if the Jiasa River Class I Hydropower Station continued, the project in question would inevitably cause the flooding of the habitats for green peafowl, a national Class I protected animal, and the biotopes for Cycas chenii, a national Class I protected plant. Undoubtedly, the wildlife and their habitats were faced with material risks posed by the construction of the involved project. In addition, in terms of the severity of the damage, the flooded areas downstream from the Jiasa River Class I Hydro power Station were abound in animal and plant species, and had considerable value of biological diversity and genetic resources; those areas were not only habitats for green peafowls, Cycas chenii, and other rare species, but also parts of a complete ecosystem together with various organisms and large areas of primitive rain forests and tropical rain forest fragments; and if the construction of the hydropower station continued, the resultant damage could be directly estimated to be irreversible. For the material risk posed, Xinping Company failed to effectively establish there was no major risk, and presented instead only the Environmental Impact Report as a rebuttal, which had insufficient probative value. Therefore, based on the preliminary results of the post-environmental impact assessment of the project ordered by the Ministry of Ecology and Environment and that the Jiasa River Class I Hydro power Station failed to take any protective measure for green peafowls during its construction, it could be determined that the continued construction of the Jiasa River Class I Hydropower Station would pose material risk to the habitat for green peafowls, the biotope for Cycas chenii, and the biological diversity and biosecurity in the entire ecosystem.

Article 27 of the Environmental Impact Assessment Law provides: "If there arises any circumstance which does not comply with the approved environmental impact assessment in the process of project construction or operation, the employer shall organize a post-environmental impact assessment evaluation, take ameliorative measures, and file them with the original authority approving the environmental impact assessment documents and the authority approving the construction project; the original authority approving the environmental impact assessment documents may order the employer to conduct a post- environmental impact assessment evaluation and take ameliorative measures." It was in compliance with the above provision for the General Office of the Ministry of Ecology and Environment to issue a Letter on Ordering Post-EIA Evaluation to Xinping Company with respect to the project in progress in this case on July 21, 2017, ordering that Xinping Company should conduct a post-environmental impact assessment of the project, take mitigation measures, and file them with the Ministry of Ecology and Environment, and should not impound water or generate power before completion of the assessment. To date, the power station involved in the case had been under suspension from construction, Xinping Company had received approval for its application to its superior authority for suspension of the construction of the project involved in the case, and the material risk posed to the ecological habitat for green peafowls had been under effective control. Under the circumstance that Xinping Company had applied for suspension of the construction of the project involved in the case, and given the fact that the Ministry of Ecology and Environment had ordered Xinping Company to conduct a post-environmental impact assessment, the level of risk for certain unclear facts, and that whether the project involved in the case might continue to be constructed, or should be canceled completely could only be determined after the decisions of the competent environmental authorities. Therefore, the follow-up actions for the project should depend on the decisions by the competent administrative authorities based on the post-EIA results.

Significance

The case is a civil preventive environmental public interest litigation for the protection of rare wildlife and plants. Preventive public interest litigation is an important example of applying the principle of prevention in environmental and resource trials. It breaks through the traditional conception of "remedy comes after damage," hence bringing ecological and environmental protection forward to an early stage in projects that may harm the environment, helping to increase the efforts of ecological and environmental protection avoiding damage to the environment altogether, or preventing further expansion of the damage. In this case, Friends of Nature has proved that if the hydropower project in question continued to be built, it would inevitably lead to the inundation of the habitat of the green peacock, a national Class I key protected animal, and the cycas chenii, a national Class I key protected plant resulting in direct and irreversible damage to biodiversity and genetic resources of the area. The People's Courts order to request Xinping Company to suspend the construction of the hydropower plant based on the existing environmental impact assessment under the law, and to complete follow-up procedures (including post-EIA) before any further decisions, provided strong judicial protection for the biodiversity of the Yangtze River basin.

Courts and Members of the Collegial Bench

Court of First Instance: In Kunming Intermediate People's Court, Yunnan, before Zheng Huili, Wang Li, Han Xiaolan, He Ying, Zhou Ruhai, Chen Jiangmei, Li Tao

Court of Second Instance: In Yunnan High People's Court, before Xiang Kai, Su Jingwei, Tian Qihui

Chapter 17
Case of Ecological and Environmental Damage Compensation Liability: Jiujiang Municipal People's Government v. Jiangxi Zhengpeng Environmental Protection Technology Co., Ltd., Hangzhou Lianxin Construction Materials Co., Ltd, Li * et 7 People

Keywords Civil/ecological · Environmental damage compensation litigation · Pre-litigation consultation · Determination of compensation liabilities

Basic Facts

Between 2017 and 2018, Jiangxi Zhengpeng Environmental Protection Technology Co., Ltd. (hereinafter referred to as "Zhengpeng Company") was contracted by Hangzhou Tangxi Thermo Power Co., Ltd. and others to transport and dispose sludge generated from their production process for disposal fees. Having acquired the sludge, Li *, the actual person-in-charge of Zhengpeng Company, directly dumped the unprocessed sludge, worked with Fengcheng Zhihe New Materials Co., Ltd. (hereinafter referred to as "Zhihe Company") in sludge dumping, or delivered the sludge to Zhang **, Shu ** et al, who had no disposal qualification, to dump sludge in multiple plots in Jiujiang City. The other company, Hangzhou Lianxin Construction Materials Co., Ltd. (hereinafter referred to as "Lianxin Company"), while knowing that Zhang ***'s engagement in illegal sludge transfer, still allowed the latter to dispose of the sludge using blank contracts with company seal. Upon appraisal, the total weight of the sludge illegally dumped was 14,800 tons, causing soil, water, and air pollution damage, and the restoration costs for such damage was assessed to be CNY 14,462,900. To hold the criminals liable, the People's Procuratorate of Xunyang District, Jiujiang City filed criminal lawsuits against Shu ** and five other defendants. The Intermediate People's Court of Jiujiang City decided in the second instance that the defendants were criminally guilty of environmental pollution and sentenced them to imprisonment ranging from two years and two months to ten months with a fine ranging from CNY 100,000 to 50,000, respectively.

Following the conclusion of the criminal trial of the case, the Jiujiang Municipal People's Government of Jiangxi Province, in accordance with the relevant provisions,

Influential Environment and Resources Cases in China (2024),
https://doi.org/10.1007/978-981-96-9562-1_17

held pre-litigation(civil) consultations with involved companies for civil compensation, and entered into compensation agreement with Hangzhou Tangxi Thermoelectricity Co., Ltd. However, the government's endeavor to reach civil compensation agreements with Zhengpeng Company, Lianxin Company, Li *, and the other six persons failed, so it proceeded to file this lawsuit and requested that all defendants perform the obligation of restoring the environment, pay the expenses for restoration of the ecological environment, extend public apologies, and bear the lawyer fee and litigation fee.

Judgment

On November 4, 2019, Intermediate People's Court of Jiujiang City, Jiangxi Province made the civil judgment (No. 201 [2019] First, Civil, 04, Jiangxi) as follows:

1. Zhengpeng Company, Li *, Huang *, Shu **, and Chen ** should jointly assume the liability for ecological restoration for the valley Plot close to Shanyan Road, Jiujiang City Economic Development Zone damaged by the sludge (Plot 3) within three months after the judgment takes effect. Should the defendants fail to implement the restoration in time, a total of CNY 2,803,396 for ecological compensation should be paid by the above defendants within 10 days starting from the end of the restoration period above (Shu ** has already paid CNY 100,000 ecological compensation fund to the Court's account).
2. Zhengpeng Company, Lianxin Company, Zhang **,Li *, Huang *, Shu **, Xia **, and Chen ** should jointly assume the liability of ecological restoration of the Zhengjiawan Plot in Wufeng Village, Shayan Road, Jiujiang City Economic Development Zone damaged by the sludge (Plot 4) within three months after this judgment takes force. Otherwise, the above defendants should pay a total of CNY 2,018,515 for ecological compensation to cover the costs needed for ecological restoration of the plot within ten days upon the end of the restoration period (Lianxin Company has already paid CNY1,000,000 as ecological restoration fund to the Court's account).
3. Zhengpeng Company, Zhang **, Li *, Xia**, and Ma ** should jointly assume the liability for ecological restoration for the Plot surrounded He Long Garden, Jiu Song Mountain in Yongxiu County, Jiujiang City damaged by the sludge (Plot 5) within three months after the judgment takes effect. Should it fail, the defendants should pay together a total of CNY 4,489,181 for ecological compensation within 10 days starting from the end of the restoration period above.
4. All defendants should jointly bear the fees for the EIA report (CNY 200,000), the Risk Assessment Plan costs (CNY 100,000), and the lawyer fees (CNY 40,000). The payment should be made within ten days after this judgment takes effect.
5. All defendants should make a public apology on media at or above provincial level within ten days after this judgment takes effect.

6. The rest of the requests by Jiujiang Municipal People's Government are dismissed.

Legal Reasoning

The court ruled that: Zhengpeng, Lianxin, Zhang **, Li *, Shu **, Huang *, Xia **, Chen **, and Ma ** caused ecological and environmental damage by colluding to illegally transfer and dump unprocessed sludge. Having harmed the public interest, they should bear the compensation for the ecological and environmental damage caused. However, since the sludge on each plot dumped by the defendants has been mixed, it is impossible for the defendants to divide the responsibility in restoring one plot. Therefore, pursuant to the principle of responsibility-sharing for joint environmental infringement, the defendants should bear joint liability for Plot 3, the sludge was collected by Li * from several companies along the Yangtze River, and dumped by Huang *, Shu ** and Chen ** together. The cost of restoration for the plot is appraised at 2,803,396 yuan, and should be borne by each of the above-mentioned defendants. Chen ** argued that he was just an employee of Li *—he received less illegal gains and played a smaller role in the illegal dumping, so that Li *, the employer, should bear the full liability or the major liability. However, the court held that the liabilities of the defendants in a joint environmental infringement case should not be determined by the size of the illegal gains or the importance of one's role in the wrongdoing. In this case, there is no evidence to prove that Chen ** was an employee of Li *, and that Chen ** did collude with the other defendants in illegal dumping of the sludge. Therefore, Chen ** should be held severally liable for environmental remediation.

For Plot 4, the sludge dumped on the plot came from Lianxin Company (acquired by Zhang ** in the name of Lianxin Company). Since Li *, Huang *, Shu ** and Chen ** colluded in the dumping, the remaining restoration cost for the Plot of CNY 2,018,515 shall be borne jointly by the above-mentioned defendants. Lianxin Company argued that the sludge dumped on the plot was from Zhang **, who could not represent Lianxin Company, and that Lianxin Company should not be liable for the compensation. However, according to evidence discovered during the trial, it is known that Lianxin Company authorized Zhang ** to use the company's official seal and blank contract for sludge disposal since the company's capacity of sludge treatment was limited, and the company did not follow relevant rules to keep track of the sludge treatment process done by Zhang **. Therefore there was obvious negligence in fulfilling its obligation of supervision by Lianxin Company; and the testimony of Zhang ** and witness Huang ** confirmed that part of the sludge of Plot 4 came from Lianxin Company. Therefore, the defense of Lianxin Company cannot be supported.

The sludge dumped on Plot 5 was sourced from Zhang ** and was dumped by Li * and Ma ** together. The cost of restoration of the plot was CNY 4,489,181, which should be borne jointly by each of the above defendants. Li *, as the actual person-in-charge of Zhengpeng Company, participated in the illegal dumping of sludge in the name of Zhengpeng Company when Zhengpeng Company had no qualification and ability to handle sludge. Hence, Li * should share the liability for ecological and environmental restoration with Zhengpeng Company together.

All the related costs claimed by the Jiujiang Municipal People's Government to be paid by the defendants including the cost of preparing the assessment report in the environmental damage appraisal report of CNY 200,000, the cost of preparing the risk assessment plan of CNY 100,000 and the lawyer fee of CNY 40,000 yuan, are reasonable expenses for the lawsuit, and should be supported. The Jiujiang Municipal People's Government's request for the defendants to make public apologies in the media at the provincial level or above is justified by law and should be supported.

Xia ** argued that he was not aware of Zhengpeng's illegal dumping of sludge and should not be held liable for ecological restoration, and that he was in the process of being prosecuted for criminal offense of environmental pollution for the same behavior, and that the criminal proceeding should take precedence over this case. However, the cooperation agreement between Zhengpeng Company and Zhihe Company (whose actual person-in-charge is Xia **), bank records and confessions of Li *, Xia **, and Zhang **, the testimony of witness Wang Dawei, and the transfer receipt of Zhihe Company are sufficient evidence to prove that Zhihe Company and Zhengpeng Company colluded in sludge dumping after the cooperation agreement signed between Zhengpeng Company and Zhihe Company on September 14, 2017, and that Xia ** obtained his share of illegal profits from sludge dumping, Xia ** should be liable for the environmental damage compensation. On the other argument, the trial of criminal cases does not always take precedence over the trial of civil cases. In this case, the facts related have already been supported by sufficient evidence, so the trial of this case does not necessarily need to be based on the results of the trial of the other criminal case, and it is not in appropriate to try this case first.

Significance

This is a case about ecological compensation for ecological and environmental damage caused by illegal dumping of industrial sludge across provinces in the Yangtze River Economic Belt. On top of holding the defendant company and individuals criminally liable, the Jiujiang Municipal People's Government fully used the instrument of ecological compensation claim procedures. First, the government tried to urge the parties liable for compensation to reach an agreement to commit to fulfill their obligation for ecological restoration and compensation through consultation; for those who failed to reach a consensus on the above compensation, the government resorted to litigation for ecological and environmental damage compensation in accordance with the law. Hence, an effective connection between pre-litigation consultation and litigation procedures is established. Moreover, the judgment of this case clearly illustrated the rule that the operator of a company should be jointly liable for letting alone illegal dumping by others, despite the fact that the operator did not directly dump the sludge themselves. If the illegal transport and dumping of sludge involves multiple parties in collusion all should be held jointly liable should it impossible to clarify the quantity of sludge dumped by each part. By doing so, the strictest legal system for ecological and environmental protection is effectively implemented.

Court and Members of the Collegial Bench

Court of First Instance: In Jiujiang Intermediate People's Court, Jiangxi, before Yan Qingyuan, Shen Shuangwu, Shi Longxi, Qian Zhenhua, Shen Ai, Zhou Hui, Xu Jun

Chapter 18
Administrative Litigation Case on Marine Animal Conservation: Hainan Lingao Yinghai Shipping Co., Ltd. v. Sansha Fishery Administration Corps

Keywords Administrative · Administrative penalty · International environmental conventions · Illegal transportation · Rare · endangered aquatic wildlife · products · Coral · Tridacnidae

Basic Facts

Tridacnidae is a type of precious clams distributed in tropical marine waters and aquatic wild animals. It is under key protection in China and the world—all nine species in Tridacnidae are listed in Appendix II of the Convention on International Trade in Endangered Species of Wild Fauna and Flora (CITES), among which Tridacna gigas is listed as China's national Class I protected animal. On August 21, 2014, the Third Coast Guard Corps of the Public Security Border Defense Unit of Hainan Province discovered during patrolling in the Sansha waters that the vessel Yiefeng 616 affiliated to Hainan Lingao Yinghai Shipping Co., Ltd. (hereinafter referred to as "Yinghai Company") the plaintiff of this case, illegally carried Tridacnidae shells in quantity. They immediately seized the vessel, and transferred the case to the Comprehensive Law Enforcement Bureau of Sansha City for handling. As the case came within the purview of the local Fishery Administration Corps (Sansha Fishery Administration Corps, the defendant of this case), the Comprehensive Law Enforcement Bureau further handed over the case to the latter.

Upon investigation, it was found that the Yinghai Company did not hold a Permit for Concessional Transportation of Aquatic Wildlife, and the vessel involved in the case carried a total of 250 tons of Tridacnidae shells. According to professional appraisal. 98% of the 250 tons of the seized Tridacnidae shells were those of Tridacna gigas, national Class I protected animals, the remaining 2% were those of hippopus, a species of Tridacnidae also listed in CITES Appendix.

Influential Environment and Resources Cases in China (2024),
https://doi.org/10.1007/978-981-96-9562-1_18

The Tridacnidae shells involved in the case worth CNY 373,500 in total. Based on the foregoing findings, the local Fishery Administration Corps made the Administrative Penalty Decision (No. 01 [2018] Fishery Administrative Penalty, Sansha, Hainan), imposing an administrative penalty on the plaintiff—confiscation of 250 tons of Tridacnidae shells and a fine three times the value of goods, i.e., CNY1.1205 million, on the grounds that Yinghai violated the Wild Animal Protection Law and other laws by transporting Tridacnidae shells by vessel Yefeng 616 without the Permit for Concessional Transportation of Aquatic Wildlife. The Company was unsatisfied and filed an administrative action with the Haikou Maritime Court, requesting revocation of the administrative penalty by the local Fishery Administration Corps.

Judgment

On November 30, 2018, the Haikou Maritime Court entered the Administrative Judgment (No. 14 [2018] First, Administrative, 72, Hainan), holding that the administrative penalty decision made by the Fishery Administration Corps of Sansha City was based on clear facts and conclusive evidence, applied laws and regulations correctly, and was in line with statutory procedures. The court dismissed the claims of Yinghai Company. Yinghai Company appealed the judgment, and the High People's Court of Hainan Province entered the Administrative Judgment (No. 125 [2019] Administrative, Final, Hainan) on April 10, 2019, dismissing the appeal and affirming the original judgment.

Legal Reasoning

The court's judgment held the following:

1. China as a party to CITES shall strictly and fully perform its obligations under the Convention, and ensure protection in accordance with the law to Anthozoa and Tridacnidae listed in Appendices I and II of the Convention, whether alive, dead, or related products. Tridacnidae is protected rare and endangered aquatic wild animals, and Tridacnidae shells are aquatic wild animal products protected by Chinese law. In accordance with paragraph 3, Article 7 of the Provisions of the Supreme People's Court on Several Issues concerning the Trial of the Relevant Cases Occurring in Sea Areas under the Jurisdiction of China (II) and Article 2 of the Regulation of the People's Republic of China on the Protection of Aquatic Wild Animals, all aquatic wild animal species under Classes I and II protection on the List of Wild Animals under State Priority Protection and those in Appendices I and II of CITES were protected by law, whether alive, dead, or related products (any parts of aquatic wild animals and their derivatives). The Tridacna gigas involved in the case was national Class I protected animal on the List of

Wild Animals under State Priority Protection, and hippopus was a species in the Appendix II of CITES, both protected by law. Although the object of transportation by Yinghai Company was Tridacnidae shells, the shells of Tridacnidae, as animals of the Bivalvia class, were parts of animals, therefore Tridacnidae shells should be identified as animal products of protected species, and should be protected under Article 2 of the Regulation of the People's Republic of China on the Protection of Aquatic Wild Animals; Yinghai Company's defense—it transported dead Tridacnidae and thus did not violate any laws and administrative regulation—was untenable.

2. Any acts of illegal catching, buying, transporting, processing, and selling of rare and endangered wild animals and their products, among others, along the industrial chain of illegal exploitation and utilization of wild animal resources should constitute violations of law, for which violators should be held liable. The illegal transport of rare and endangered wildlife and their products involved in this case was an important link of the illegal supply chain the transporters should bear corresponding legal consequences and liability. Pursuant to Article 23 of the Wild Animal Protection Law of China as revised on August 27, 2009, Article 20 of the Regulation of the People's Republic of China on the Protection of Aquatic Wild Animals, and Article 29 of the Measures of the People's Republic of China for Special Lice rises for Exploitation of Aquatic Wild Animals, in force at the time of the case, any transportation and carrying of wild animals under state priority protection or their products across county borders should be subject to the approval with permits by the wildlife protection authorities of provincial level governments or the entities authorized by the provincial competent governments (province, autonomous regions, and municipalities). In this case, Yinghai Company violated the law by transporting the Tridacnidae shells involved in the case from Sansha City to Hainan Island without approval or any permits, the imposition of a fine on it by the Fishery Administration Corps of Sansha City was in compliance with relevant laws and administrative regulations.

Significance

The "Yefeng 616" ship seized by the local law enforcement authority was located in the sea near the north of Zhongjian Island, Sansha City and was under the jurisdiction of the Haikou Maritime Court. The Tridacna shells involved in the case is national Class I and II protected aquatic wildlife—the people's court, through appropriate application of national laws and judicial interpretations, effectively implemented CITES, and ensured all species listed in the Convention's appendix, be them live, dead, products, or derivatives were equally protected. The judgment also made it clear that all links of the illegal industry chain that damaged the biological resources should be cracked down, and the authority of the administrative law enforcement department was vigorously safeguarded. It demonstrates the commitment of the judicial and administrative organs to cooperate in combating illegal transportation of aquatic wildlife under national protection, maintaining marine biodiversity and ecological security.

Courts and Members of the Collegial Bench

Court of First Instance: In Haikou Maritime Court, before Jiao Nan, Zeng Jianhua, Zhang Yifang

Court of Second Instance: In Hainan High People's Court, before Wang Jun, Zhang Shuang, Feng Kun

Chapter 19
Administrative Litigation Case on Shoreline Protection: Beihai Naizhi Ocean Technology Co., Ltd. v. Ocean and Fishery Bureau of Beihai City

Keywords Administrative · Administrative penalty · Illegal enclosure and reclamation · Coastline protection · Marine environment · Determination of liabilities in joint illegal acts · Lenient and lesser administrative penalty

Basic Facts

Beihai Naizhi Ocean Technology Co., Ltd. (hereinafter referred to as "Naizhi Company") filed a case to the people's court, alleging that the Ocean and Fishery Bureau of Beihai City (hereinafter referred to as the "Ocean and Fishery Bureau"), the local fishery authority, was inappropriate in making its administrative penalty decision against the company which requested Naizhi Company to pay a fine for its illegal enclosure and reclamation of 0.38 hectares of sea areas, which was 15 times of the marine space utilization charge for the area they occupied. The plaintiff found the decision lacked factual and legal basis, and was more severe than it needed to be, therefore requested revocation of the administrative penalty decision. Naizhi Company claimed that, it did not performed any acts of reclamation itself, instead, it was Beihai Yufeng Marine Aquaculture Co., Ltd. (hereinafter referred to as "Yufeng Company") who reclaimed the sea area at first; and that even if Naizhi Company did commit the illegal act of reclamation, as Naizhi Company and Yufeng Company both performed reclamation in the same sea area, both violators should jointly be liable, and Naizhi Company should be given a lighter or mitigated penalty.

The Ocean and Fishery Bureau defended that it was established by the transcripts of on-site investigation, photos, and other evidence that Naizhi Company did perform the act of reclamation and that it had respectively investigated and imposed punishment on both Naizhi Company and Yufeng Company for their illegal acts, and the penalty payable determined for Naizhi Company was in line with relevant laws.

Influential Environment and Resources Cases in China (2024),
https://doi.org/10.1007/978-981-96-9562-1_19

The court ascertained the following facts upon trial: On June 1, 2013, Yufeng Company and Shitoubu Village Group, Xinggang Town, Tieshangang District, Beihai City signed a Rural Land Lease Contract, stipulating that the Shitoubu Village Group would lease the vacant plot of land located on the seaside of Shitoubu Village, adjacent to the harbor on the left and the Beilin Wharf on the right, in parallel with the seafront road, 100 meters along the road, 145 meters into the sea, a total of 21.78 mu (Chinese unit of land measurement that is 0.165 acre) in extent, to Yufeng Company for management and use as a venue for seafood freezing. It was also found that the seaside vacant land above leased under the contract was actually located off the coastline. From July to September of the same year, Yufeng Company hired others to extract sea sand and reclaim it in the involved sea area to form a mound of sand. On May 12, 2016, Naizhi Company and Yufeng Company signed an Agreement on the Assignment of a Contract for Land Usufruct, and Naizhi Company acquired the rights of Yufeng Company under the original contract. From July to September of the same year, Naizhi Company used machinery and vehicles to transport soil and construction waste to level the seaside vacant land it leased (actually tidelands), built a temporary wharf, created a land area, and prepared to build a cool store, without acquiring the right to use the sea area in accordance with the law.

In October 2017, the Ocean and Fishery Bureau filed a case to investigate and handle the reclamation and construction on the area, and found the sea area illegally occupied by Naizhi Company was 0.38 hectares. After hearing Naizhi's statement of defenses, a public hearing and two joint review meetings, the Ocean and Fishery Bureau made the Administrative Penalty Decision (No. 09 [2017] Penalty, Fishery, Beihai), ordering it to return the illegally occupied sea area, restoring the sea area to its original state, and imposing a fine of CNY 2.5677 million, i.e., 15 times the cost of marine space utilization charge to compensate the cost for the period of illegal occupation of the sea area. Naizhi Company was dissatisfied, and filed an administrative action, requesting revocation of the administrative penalty decision.

Judgment

The Beihai Maritime Court entered the Administrative Judgment (No. 2 [2018] First, Administrative, 72, Guangxi) on September 17, 2018, dismissing the claims of the plaintiff. Naizhi Company appealed after the judgment was pronounced. On June 26, 2019, the High People's Court of Guangxi Zhuang Autonomous Region entered the Administrative Judgment (No. 1163 [2018] Final, Administrative, Guangxi), dismissing the appeal and affirming the original judgment.

Legal Reasoning

The court's effective judgment held the following: The seaside vacant land occupied by Naizhi Company was on the seaward side of the coastline (natural coastline), and was actually seaside tidelands. Naizhi Company used its own forklifts, hook lifts, and other machinery, as well as soil and construction waste from elsewhere, to level and rein force the mound of sand which Yufeng Company created by dredging, built a temporary wharf, and filled another sea area in the southwest of the temporary wharf to build sandbag cofferdams and dike protection facilities on the north seaward side of the temporary wharf. The above acts of leveling and filling the grounds and building cofferdams for dike protection resulted in changes of the natural attributes of the sea area and formation of a new coastline and were acts of reclamation. Naizhi Company performed reclamation on the 0.38-hectare sea area involved in the case without acquiring a lawful right to use the area, it constituted illegal reclamation.

Both Yufeng Company and Naizhi Company conducted certain reclamation activities in the sea area involved in the case, but their illegal acts were separable and in dependent, and were not joint illegal acts. First, Yufeng Company and Naizhi Company neither had the intention to jointly commit illegal acts nor jointly committed the illegal acts. In terms of time, Yufeng Company hired others to extract sea sand and place it in the sea area involved in the case to build a mound of sand, from July to September 2013. Naizhi Company acquired the rights of Yufeng Company under the original contract by signing an assignment agreement on May 12, 2016, and leveled the sea area involved in the case to build a temporary wharf and form a land area from July to September 2016. Their reclamation activities were relatively remote from and independent of each other; and there was no cooperation. Second, the violations by Yufeng Company and Naizhi Company were different in nature. Yufeng Company only extracted sea sand and placed it in the sea area involved in the case to build a mound of sand, and its violation was relatively minor in degree. Naizhi Company conducted cofferdam building and ground leveling in the sea area involved in the case, built a temporary wharf, and created a land area. Its acts of violation were more serious and were more execrable by nature. Third, the acts by Yufeng Company and Naizhi Company resulted in different consequences. Yufeng Company had not completely changed the marine environment of the sea area involved in the case by its acts; Naizhi Company conducted cofferdam building and grounds leveling in the sea area involved in the case, built a temporary wharf, and created a new land area, and its acts resulted in complete changes in the marine ecology and environment of the sea area involved, constituted illegal reclamation, and caused more serious harmful consequences. The Ocean and Fishery Bureau determined that the illegal acts of Naizhi Company and Yufeng Company were independent of each other, and filed cases separately for investigation and handling. That had factual and legal basis and was not improper. Naizhi Company's defenses—the Ocean and Fishery Bureau selectively took law enforcement actions and Yufeng Company should be jointly liable with it—were untenable. As Naizhi Company did not voluntarily take any measures to reduce or eliminate the harmful consequences of reclamation even after its illegal acts were found and investigated, it fell outside of the circumstances for a lighter or mitigated penalty—Naizhi Company's request for a lighter or mitigated administrative penalty had no legal basis. Naizhi Company leveled, enclosed, and filled the sea area involved in the case, and the total reclaimed area was 0.38 hectares. Its acts resulted in changes in the natural attributes of the sea area and formation of a new land area, and adversely affected the coastal ecology. The Ocean and Fishery Bureau's decision to impose a fine, i.e., 15 times the cost of the marine space utilization charge, was in accordance with Article 42 of the Law on the Administration of Sea Areas, which provided "a fine of not less than ten times nor more than 20 times the cost of use of the sea area payable according to the size of the sea areas for the period of illegal use." The fine did not violate the provisions of the Administrative Penalty Law on the application of administrative Penalty Law on the application of administrative penalties, and was a reasonable penalty within the range of administrative penalties under the Several Opinions of the China Marine Surveillance on Further Regulating the Exercise of Discretion over Maritime Administrative Penalties, rather than a penalty heavier than necessary. In conclusion, with regard to the penalty to impose a fine of CNY2.5677 million, the facts found were clear, and the application of the law was not improper.

Significance

This is a case of marine administrative penalty involving illegal sea enclosures and reclamation. With the development of China's marine economy and the improvement of people's living standards, the demand for sea use by entities and individuals engaged in marine industries has grown rapidly. It has been found that some companies and individuals, without obtaining the right to use the sea, illegally enclose the sea, occupy the sea or even conduct reclamation, causing serious impact on marine ecology and sustainable development. China's coastline is long, and sometimes it is difficult to investigate, punish, and enforce illegal acts of sea use for administrative departments. The handling of this case sets a precedence for several key issues such as the identification of the subject of illegal sea enclosure and reclamation, the due process of administrative penalties, and the exercise of administrative discretion. It fully demonstrates the commitment of the People's Court to protect the national coastline and the security of marine ecology with the strictest system and rule of law, and is of significance in advocating for using and managing the sea in accordance with the law.

Courts and Members of the Collegial Bench

Court of First Instance: In Beihai Maritime Court, before Qiu Deping, Lu Yingtao, Lao Jianming

Court of Second Instance: In Guangxi High People's Court, before Zhang Hui, Xiong Mei, Jiang Xinjiang

Chapter 20
Administrative Public Interest Litigation Case of Administrative Failure to Protect the Environment and Prevent Pollution: People's Procuratorate of Sanyuan County, Shaanxi Province v. People's Government of * Town, Sanyuan County, Shaanxi Province

Keywords Administrative · Environmental public interest litigation · Damage to social · Public interests · Major risks

Basic Facts

In 2012, the defendant, the people's government of a town in Sanyuan County Shaanxi (hereinafter referred to as the town government) laid a subsurface drainage system to transport sewage from the four villages and seven companies in the eastern town to a central treatment which used to be a drainage trench leading to Qing River in the southern Dacheng Village back in the 1960s. In an attempt to improve the town's environment and prevent untreated sewage discharges, the town government submitted the "Proposed Project of Building Sewage Treatment Plant and Network in ** Town to Sanyuan Development and Reform Bureau, Xian yang Ecology and Environment Bureau (Sanyuan Branch) (formerly Sanyuan Environmental Protection Bureau), Sanyuan Natural Resource Bureau (formerly Sanyuan Land and Resource Bureau), Sanyuan Housing and Urban-Rural Development Bureau which all gave the project the green light." On April 15, 2016, Sanyuan People's Procuratorate issued a "Procuratorial Recommendation" to the town government to urge the latter to "perform its duty to improve environmental quality according to the law, build sewage treatment facilities and supporting pipeline network to ensure that the sewage discharged into the Qing River is up to the national standards."

The town government did not reply within the required timeframe, nor did it start the construction of the sewage treatment plant and the sewage network. Later, Sanyuan People's Procuratorate commissioned Xi'an Yuchi Testing Technology Co., Ltd. to test the sewage discharged from the outlet. The results from the separate tests on June 20, June 22, and July 4, 2016, revealed that the concentration of BOD5,

Influential Environment and Resources Cases in China (2024),
https://doi.org/10.1007/978-981-96-9562-1_20

CODcr, ammonia nitrogen, and suspended solids in the sewage exceeded the standards for the Yellow River Basin (Shaanxi section) and the national grade 1 standard (GB8978-1996), meaning the sewage problem remained unsolved. On October 24, 2016, Sanyuan People's Procuratorate filed a public interest lawsuit with Sanyuan People's Court, requesting a court order to confirm the town government failure to perform its environmental protection and pollution prevention duties in accordance with the law regarding the sewage discharge in the southern part of Dacheng Village; it further requested that the town government continue to perform its statutory duties and build sewage treatment facilities and pipeline networks to ensure that the sewage discharged into Qinghe River met the relevant standards.

In its defense, the town government argued it had submitted the project to the Sanyuan Development and Reform Bureau, Xianyang Ecological and Environmental Bureau (Sanyuan Branch). Sanyuan Natural Resource Bureau, Sanyuan Housing and Urban-Rural Development Bureau and obtained approval; the land acquisition procedure had been finished and the construction could start any time. In the meanwhile, in early 2016, the government declared the national key "Three-year Rotating Plan Project," and the construction procedure had been completed. The government argued that it had performed its duties in accordance with the law before receiving Sanyuan People's Procuratorate's recommendations on April 15, 2016. In the submission for approval, the town government mentioned in the feasibility report that the construction length was 25 months.

Judgment

Sanyuan People's Court made a judgment on April 11, 2017 (No.21 [2016] First, Administrative, 0422, Shaanxi):

a. confirmed the fact that the town government was responsible for the substandard sewage discharge through the southern outfall and failed to fully perform the statutory environmental protection and pollution prevention duties; its acts were illegal; b. the town government should construct and complete the sewer network and centralized sewage treatment facilities within 25 months after the effective date of this judgment to ensure that the sewage discharged into the Qinghe River meet the discharge standards.

Legal Reasoning

The court held that the area under the jurisdiction of the town government is located along the northern coast of the Qinghe River, a tributary of the Weihe River, and therefore it is the government's legal duty to build a sewer network and a central treatment in rural areas as stipulated in the "Shaanxi Weihe Watershed Management Regulations." The town government applied to the relevant departments to improve the local environment as early as 2012, and its submission of "Proposed Project of Building Sewage Treatment Plant and Network in ** Town" was approved by Sanyuan Development and Reform Bureau, Xianyang Ecological and Environmental Bureau (Sanyuan Branch), Sanyuan Natural Resource Bureau. Sanyuan Housing and Urban-Rural Development Bureau, meaning the government obtained the construction approval, environmental impact approval, and land approval for the proposed project and completed the site selection for the proposed project. But four years went by, the government has not yet started the construction. The sewage from the four villages and seven companies had been discharged untreated into the Qing River through the southern outlet in Dacheng Village, affecting the production activities, quality of life and the environment in surrounding communities. The government failed to fix the problem even after receiving the "Procuratorial Recommendations," leaving the public interest in harm's way. Therefore, the town government's inaction has constituted negligence in performing its statutory duties.

The only finished procedure was land acquisition for the sewage treatment plant, and the construction of other sewage treatment facilities and sewer network projects was put on hold. As the statutory administrative department in charge of the construction of rural sewer networks and centralized sewage treatment facilities within its jurisdiction and of rural environmental protection, the town government should proceed with its statutory duties of constructing sewage treatment facilities and sewer networks in accordance with the law, and take effective measures to ensure that the sewage discharge within the jurisdiction of the town meets the relevant standards. Given the affected scope and the sheer workload of the project, the town government mentioned in the feasibility study report during the submission that the project would be completed in 25 months, which was a reasonable project life and was implementable according to the feasibility study. In the end, Sanyuan People's Court of confirmed that the act of the town government was illegal and ordered it to perform its duties within 25 months after the verdict came into effect. Neither parties appealed against the verdict of the first instance.

Significance

This is a case of administrative public interest litigation arising from the construction of rural centralized sewage treatment sewer networks in the Yellow River Watershed. Sewage treatment facilities and pipe networks in rural areas are vital to water pollution prevention and play an important role in creating a livable and beautiful countryside. In this case, the town government failed to perform its statutory duties and moved slowly with the construction of the project after obtaining the approval, resulting in long-term untreated sewage discharge into the Qinghe River. The people's court uphold the claim of the procuratorial organ and after the judgment took effect, joined the procuratorial organ in site inspection to keep track of the progress of the project and urged for operation of the facilities as scheduled. The efforts of the people's court have demonstrated that in addressing the most pressing environmental challenges in rural areas and implementing the strategy of rural revitalization, the judicial system is dedicated to safeguarding public interests by giving full play to judicial functions and upholding law-based administration.

Court and Members of the Collegial Bench

Court of First Instance: In Sanyuan Primary People's Court, Shaanxi, before Quan Junxi, Wang Jingfeng, Sun Fangfang

Chapter 21
Criminal and Collateral Civil Public Interest Litigation Against Qin * Xue for Illegal Logging

Keywords Criminal · The crime of illegal logging · Ecological restoration · Replanting · Expert opinion · Bond

Key Points

1. In determining a defendant's obligation to restore a forest ecological system, the court may refer to opinions from experts and forestry planning and environmental protection authorities. Courts may order the type, age, number, and location of trees to be planted, as well as the required survival rate and any deadline for compliance.
2. Where the defendant voluntarily pays a bond to ensure compliance with their ecological restoration obligation, courts may consider this a mitigating factor.

Basic Facts

The Baojing County People's Procuratorate in Hunan Province (Procuratorate) charged the defendant Qin * Xue with the crime of illegal logging and brought this case before the Baojing County People's Court (court). During the trial, a collateral civil public interest action was also brought on the grounds that public interests had been harmed.

The Procuratorate submitted that the defendant should bear criminal liability for the offense of illegal logging; and that since the defendant's actions had severely damaged the ecological environment and harmed the public interest, relevant provisions of the Tort Liability Law provide that the defendant should undertake reforestation and make a public apology. While conceding liability, the defendant pleaded

Influential Environment and Resources Cases in China (2024),
https://doi.org/10.1007/978-981-96-9562-1_21

in mitigation of sentence that as owner and operator of the land, he had already paid the reforestation bond.

At the hearing, the court found that the Mount Baiyun county-level Nature Reserve had been established in 1998. It was centered around the Mount Baiyun County state-owned forest farm, which had been established in 1958. The Reserve was accorded provincial status in 2005 when the public interest forest area was delineated; then in 2013 it was named a National Nature Reserve. In 1998, the defendant won a contract for the Tudi'ao section of forest in the heart of the Reserve, in Wodang Village, Maogou Township, Baojing County. In 1999, the defendant began planting fir trees on land within the public interest forest area. From September 2016 to January 2017, the defendant illegally felled and sold fir trees on this parcel of land, without a logging permit and in violation of the Forestry Law. Some117.5 mu (1 mu is approximately 666.7 m^2) of the felled area were within the core section of this protected land, while 15.46 mu were outside. In total, the defendant felled 1010 trees amounting to more than 153 cubic meters (m^3) of vegetation. The Baojing County Forest Planning and Surveying Team certified that replanting saplings to replace the felled trees would cost CNY66,025.

During the hearing, the Baojing County Forest Planning and Surveying Team, together with the county forestry bureau and the Reserve, proposed specific recommendations and expert requirements for replanting the damaged area. To guarantee the fulfillment of his obligation, the defendant paid a bond of CNY66,025.

Judgment

On August 3, 2018, the Baojing County People's Court in Hunan issued the [2018, Hunan, 3125, Criminal First Trial, No. 5] Joint Civil and Criminal Judgment.

It found the defendant guilty of illegal logging, sentencing him to 3 years' imprisonment and 4 years' probation, plus a fine of CNY10,000. The court also ordered the defendant to replant 5050 one-year-old fir saplings in the Tudi'ao area of the Reserve within 2 years, and directed that the saplings should have a minimum survival rate of 90%. The defendant did not appeal, and the first-instance judgment was executed.

Complying with his sentence, the defendant planted 5050 one-year-old fir saplings on the land where logging had occurred, with a 100% survival rate.

Reasoning

The court found the defendant guilty of illegal logging for the unlicensed mass-felling of trees on public interest land within the core section of the Reserve. This logging violated the Forestry Law and occurred without the consent of forestry authorities. The defendant's contrition as a first-time offender admitting the charges, and his replanting bond of CNY66,025 paid into court, were taken into consideration as mitigating factors enabling the court to pass a more lenient sentence.

The Reserve is located within one of China's 17 key biodiversity areas, namely the Wuling Mountains and the You River Delta. It serves as an important channel for the flow of flora and fauna between the Yunnan-Guizhou Plateau, the Sichuan Basin, the Xuefeng Ranges, and the Xiangzhong Basin. Moreover, the Reserve is also a key water resources conservation area of the Yuan River, a tributary of the Dongting Lake in the Yangtze River basin. Its forests serve many crucial functions, including soil and water conservation, and the maintenance of biodiversity.

The trees purchased, planted, and managed by the defendant had already become an inseparable and organic component of the Mount Baiyun Nature Reserve's forestry resources. The defendant's unlicensed felling of the trees constituted a tortious act, as it severely disrupted the Reserve's ecosystem, endangered biodiversity, and seriously harmed the public interest. However, collateral civil public interest litigation is not a conventional civil action; nor is the Procuratorate as plaintiff a victim in the traditional sense of the word. The court granted the plaintiff's request that the defendant bear legal liability for replanting the affected area and restoring it to its pre-logging condition, as the request was deemed rational and well-founded in law and evidence. In particular, the Tudi'ao replanting plan prepared by the Baojing County Forest Planning and Surveying Team, with expert material and opinions provided by the county forestry bureau and the Mount Baiyun Nature Reserve, and Article 39(2) of the Forestry Law, all supported the plaintiff's request that the defendant bear responsibility for replanting.

Counsel for the defendant submitted that his right to operate the contracted land should also be accorded lawful protection; this was also held to be reasonable and taken into account in determining the defendant's liability.

Court and Members of the Collegial Bench

Court of First Instance: In Baojing Primary People's Court, Hunan, before Long Ouling, Xu Yansong, Xiang Fusheng, Peng Fei, Peng Juzhong, Peng Dajiang, Jia Changjin

Chapter 22
Case Against Li *, He * Min, Zhang * Bo, and Others for Disrupting Computer Information Systems

Keywords Criminal · Crime of disrupting computer information systems · Interfering with environmental quality monitoring sampling · Data distortion · Severe consequences

Key Points
Environmental quality monitoring systems are a type of computer information system. The act of obstructing such equipment with cotton yarn and other materials, thereby interfering with sampling and causing severe data distortions, constitutes the crime of disrupting computer information systems.

Basic Facts

The automated environmental air quality monitoring substation in the Chang'an district of Xi'an (substation) is one of the city's 13 state-controlled stations certified by the Ministry of Environmental Protection (MEP). It collects and sorts air quality data automatically, transmitting information to the China Environmental Monitoring Centre (Centre) every hour for live publication online. This data is also used to compile monthly, quarterly, and annual national air quality bulletins for nationwide publication. The substation is one of two municipal substations under direct state monitoring, with maintenance contracted out by the MEP to a Wuhan environmental protection company. Unauthorized access is forbidden. On February 4, 2016, the substation was relocated to the roof of the Kinetics Building on the southern campus

Influential Environment and Resources Cases in China (2024),
https://doi.org/10.1007/978-981-96-9562-1_22

of the Xi'an University for Posts and Communications in the city's Chang'an district. Defendant Li * took advantage of this relocation to intercept the substation's key and memorize the password to its monitors. From March to June 2016, defendants Li * and Zhang * Bo repeatedly accessed the substation, stuffing its sampling machines with cotton yarn to interfere with the data-collecting capacity of the automated air quality monitoring system. Despite having full knowledge of the duo's actions, defendant He * Min failed to intervene, requesting simply that the air pollution index be lowered. On several occasions, defendant Li * instructed defendants Zhang * 1 and Zhang * 2 to interfere with the substation's automated monitoring system by using the same method. This caused repeated anomalies with severe distortions in the data over several monitoring periods, disrupting normal operations of the national air quality monitoring system. Trying to cover their tracks, defendants Zhang * 1 and Zhang * 2 acted on defendant Li*'s instructions, accessing the substation on 7 and 9 March to delete surveillance footage. In February and March 2016, data from the substation had already been transmitted live to the Centre every hour, published to society at large, and used to compile the MEP's air quality assessment and rankings for 74 cities in February/March and the first quarter of 2016.

During an audit on March 5, 2016, the Centre found unusually low figures from the substation, leading it to uncover the data fabrication. Police arrested the five defendants Li *, He * Min, Zhang * 1, Zhang * 2, and Zhang * Bo. All defendants admitted the charges—except for He * Min, who argued that he only acquiesced to interference with the monitors, and should be found not guilty.

Judgment

On June 15, 2017, the Xi'an Intermediate People's Court in Shaanxi Province delivered the [2016, Shaanxi, 01, Criminal First Trial, No. 233] Criminal Judgment.

For the crime of disrupting computer systems, the court imposed custodial sentences on all five defendants:

(i) Li*: 22 months' imprisonment
(ii) He * Min: 19 months' imprisonment
(iii) Zhang * Bo: 16 months' imprisonment
(iv) Zhang * 1: 15 months' imprisonment
(v) Zhang * 2: 15 months' imprisonment

None of the defendants appealed.

Reasoning

The court held that all five defendants breached state regulations. Article 68 of the Environmental Protection Law of the People's Republic of China (EPL) forbids altering or forging monitoring data or instructing others to do the same, while Article 126 of the Atmospheric Pollution Prevention and Control Law of the People's Republic of China prohibits deceit or trickery in air quality monitoring. Article 7 of the Rules for Protecting Environmental Computer Systems of the People's Republic of China provides that the safety of computer information systems is inviolable. All five defendants fabricated monitoring data by obstructing the sampling machines or instructing others to do the same, thereby violating the state regulations. The actions of all five defendants constituted disruption of computer systems. Article 11 of the Judicial Interpretation of the Supreme People's Court and the Supreme People's Procuratorate on Issues of Applicable Law in Trying Criminal Cases of Harming Computer Information Systems provides that computer systems and computer information systems refer to systems capable of automatic data processing and include computers, online equipment, communications equipment, and automated equipment.

Article 10(1) of the Judicial Interpretation of the Supreme People's Court and the Supreme People's Procuratorate on Issues of Applicable Law in Trying Criminal Cases of Environmental Pollution provides that interfering with the sampling of environmental quality monitoring systems to cause severe data distortion constitutes disruption of computer information systems. The substation was a state-controlled automated air quality monitoring station whose figures were relayed by system software to the Centre and published via official government websites of the MEP and Centre. Publication of such air quality data was in real-time.

The sampling machine was an integral part of the air quality monitoring system; its PM10 and PM2.5 data were two of the most important indicators in assessing air pollution. The defendants' actions in dismantling or obstructing the sampling machines with cotton yarn had the natural consequence of affecting airflow throughout the machines, distorting the monitoring data, and interfering with a correct assessment of air pollution. Such interference caused the computer information systems to malfunction. The actions of all five defendants had severe consequences.

Firstly: defendants Li *, Zhang * Bo, Zhang * 1, and Zhang * 2 repeatedly interfered with sampling by obstructing or dismantling the sampling machines. Meanwhile, while fully aware of the others' actions, defendant He * Min did nothing to stop them, and simply requested that Li * lower the air pollution index.

Secondly: the defendants' interference caused markedly abnormal readings, so from February to March 2016, the substation reported data on particulates that did not conform to fluctuation patterns reported by neighboring substations: its PM2.5 data displayed anomalies from 6 p.m. on 24 February to 4 p.m. on 25 February, and from 4 a.m. on 3 March to 7 p.m. on 6 March; its PM10 data displayed anomalies from 6 p.m. on 18 February to 8 a.m. on 19 February, from 8 a.m. on 21 February to 8 p.m. on 25 February, and from 7 p.m. on 5 March to 11 p.m. on 6 March.

The substation's PM10 data reported a 41% decrease from 361 to 213 between 7 p.m. and 10 p.m. on March 5, 2016, while nearby substations reported an average 14% increase from 316 to 361. From 4 p.m. to 5 p.m. on 6 March, the substation reported an increase of 127% from 188 to 426, while others reported minor fluctuations, down to 310 from 318. Between 5 p.m. and 7 p.m. on 6 March, the substation reported a 27% drop from 426 to 309, while the others reported negligible changes (from 310 to 304). It was therefore clear that the defendants' actions in obstructing the sampling machines caused severe data distortion, as noted in the markedly low readings uncovered by the Centre during a routine audit.

Thirdly: the distorted data had already been reported to the Centre in real-time, and published to society at large. Average hourly readings from the substation had already been reported live online.

Fourthly: the distorted data had already been used to compile monthly and quarterly environmental assessments. The MEP used the distorted data in compiling its air quality rankings for 74 key cities in February/March 2016 and for the first quarter of 2016, which in turn had been published and reported to the State Council. The distorted data impacted the country's air quality control assessment and the credibility of the Government of the People's Republic of China; it also misinformed environmental decision-making. The five defendants' actions in interfering with the sampling thus satisfied the requirement of "severe consequences" in Article 286 of the Criminal Law.

All five defendants were convicted of the crime of disrupting computer information systems. However, the court accepted more lenient sentences could be passed, given their confessions and contrite behavior after arrest.

Court and Members of the Collegial Bench

Court of First Instance: In Xi'an Intermediate People's Court, Shaanxi, before Zhang Yanping, Luo Chengxing, Yuan Bing

Chapter 23
Case Against Wang * Cheng and Others for Illegally Trading and Storing Hazardous Substances

Keywords Criminal · Illegally trading or storing hazardous substances · Toxic substances

Key Points

1. The state strictly monitors and controls toxic substances that pose grave danger to human health and the environment—such as sodium cyanide, which can poison or kill people. Such substances fall within the definition of "toxic" under Article 125(2) of the Criminal Law.
2. The act of "illegally trading" toxic substances refers to buying or selling toxic substances in violation of laws and agency regulations; it does not require buying and selling.

Basic Facts

The prosecution argued that the defendants, Wang * Cheng, Jin * Miao, Sun * Fa, Zhong * Dong, and Zhou * Ming, conspired to endanger public safety by illegally purchasing sodium cyanide. Although such actions should result in criminal liability for illegally trading toxic substances, the prosecution recommended lesser, suspended sentences because the defendants truthfully confessed to their crimes. They had also purchased the sodium cyanide for electroplating purposes, and no serious consequences ensued.

Counsel for Wang * Cheng submitted (i) sodium cyanide is a toxic chemical the use of which is restricted, not prohibited, so it does not belong to the category of poisonous substances; (ii) the conduct of Wang * Cheng and others in purchasing

Influential Environment and Resources Cases in China (2024),
https://doi.org/10.1007/978-981-96-9562-1_23

sodium cyanide without authorization does not satisfy the requirements of Article 125(2) of the Criminal Law; and (iii) as no serious consequences ensued, Wang * Cheng should be found not guilty.

The court found that defendants Wang * Cheng and Jin * Miao, who were unauthorized to purchase or use acutely toxic chemicals, made a contract that Wang * Cheng should purchase sodium cyanide. From October 2006 to the end of 2007, he bought three lots of sodium cyanide from Ni Ronghua (prosecuted separately) for CNY1000 per barrel, paying a total of CNY40,000. From August 2008 to September 2009, he bought three lots of sodium cyanide from Li Guangming (prosecuted separately) for CNY975 per bag, paying a total of CNY117,000.

Wang * Cheng and Jin * Miao stored the sodium cyanide in the locked warehouses of their workshops in a hardware company in Shaoxing, Zhejiang, and used the substance for electroplating production.

Wang * Cheng used one-third of the total amount, while Jin * Miao used two-thirds. In May 2008 and July 2009, respectively, defendant Sun * Fa purchased one barrel and one bag of sodium cyanide from Wang * Cheng for CNY2000. In July and August 2008, defendant Zhong * Dong bought five bags of sodium cyanide from Wang * Cheng for CNY1000 per bag. In September 2009, defendant Zhou * Ming bought three bags of sodium cyanide from Wang * Cheng for CNY1000 per bag.

Sun * Fa, Zhong * Dong, and Zhou * Ming stored the sodium cyanide in their locked warehouses, or in their respective workshops' water troughs, and used the material for electroplating production.

Judgment

On March 31, 2012, the Yuecheng District People's Court in Shaoxing, Zhejiang issued the [2011, Shaoxing Yuecheng, Criminal First Trial, No. 205] Criminal Judgment. The court imposed suspended custodial sentences on all five defendants for illegally trading and storing hazardous substances:

(i) Wang * Cheng: 3 years' imprisonment, suspended for 5 years
(ii) Jin * Miao: 3 years' imprisonment, suspended for 4 years and 6 months
(iii) Zhong * Dong: 3 years' imprisonment, suspended for 4 years
(iv) Zhou * Ming: 3 years' imprisonment, suspended for 3 years and 6 months
(v) Sun * Fa: 3 years' imprisonment, suspended for 3 years

None of the defendants appealed.

Reasoning

The court found that all defendants had failed to obtain permits to use acutely toxic chemicals, and had violated regulations including the State Council's Regulations for the Safe Management of Hazardous Chemicals, by illegally purchasing and storing sodium cyanide despite knowing it to be a toxic chemical. Their actions constituted the crime of illegally trading and storing hazardous substances, and all five defendants were joint offenders.

Rejecting counsel's submissions on behalf of Wang * Cheng, the court held that although sodium cyanide was not a prohibited toxic chemical, it was restricted in the Catalog of Hazardous Chemicals. Sodium cyanide may cause poisoning or death, so it is highly toxic and hazardous to humans and the environment. As such, it falls under the definition of "toxic" substances in Article 125(2) of the Criminal Law.

The act of "illegally trading" toxic substances refers to the unauthorized act of buying or selling toxic substances in violation of laws and departmental regulations; it does not require buying and selling.

The defendants were not qualified to purchase or store sodium cyanide. Despite this, they violated state regulations and illegally bought and sold large amounts of toxic chemicals, evading official monitoring, disrupting the management regime for hazardous chemicals, and inflicting material harm on the lives, health, and property of the public. This was deemed sufficient to harm public safety, so the defendants' actions constituted the crime of illegally trading and storing hazardous substances.

Following their arrests, all defendants confessed to their crimes, and as the sodium cyanide was used for electroplating production with no serious consequences, the court accepted they could be dealt with more leniently. In such circumstances, including the defendants' contrition and other factors, suspended sentences were possible. The prosecution's sentencing recommendations, and the pleas of Wang * Cheng, Zhong * Dong, and Zhou * Ming for lesser sentences, were accepted.

Court and Members of the Collegial Bench

Court of First Instance: In Yuecheng Primary People's Court, Zhejiang, before Fu Yingying, Chen Jianhua, Li Li

Chapter 24
Lv * Kui and 78 Others vs. Shanhaiguan Industry Co., Ltd. Over Liability for Marine Pollution

Keywords Civil · Liability for marine pollution damage · Standards for discharge of pollutants

Key Points
According to the Marine Environmental Protection Law of the People's Republic of China and other regulations, "pollutants" that cause marine environmental pollution are not limited to substances explicitly listed in national or local environmental standards. If sewage discharged into seawater contains iron or other components not so listed, causing damage to fishery producers' aquaculture, the polluter shall bear environmental tort liability.

Basic Facts

On August 2, 2010, seawater in the eastern area of Laolongtou, Shanhaiguan District, Qinhuangdao, was found abnormal. At 11:30 a.m., after receiving a tip-off about this abnormality, the Municipal Ecology and Environment Bureau of Qinhuangdao (EEB) sent environmental monitoring staff to the site, to work with the Deputy Party Secretary and the Secretary of the Committee for Discipline Inspection of Shanhaiguan District, as well as other personnel, in inspecting the coastal environment. During the inspection, they found the seawater was reddish-brown and turbid. The EEB staff took samples of this water for testing, and reported findings on 3 August. Their analysis revealed the seawater was highly alkaline, with a pH of 8.28, and among other contaminants, its iron concentration was 13.1 milligrams per liter (mg/L).

Influential Environment and Resources Cases in China (2024),
https://doi.org/10.1007/978-981-96-9562-1_24

The court commissioned the Institute of Maritime Forensic Sciences of Dalian Maritime University (IMFS) to conduct a judicial appraisal of the pollution, and the aquaculture losses it caused.

To identify causes of this pollution, the IMFS reviewed satellite remote sensing technology and selected two images taken by a National Oceanic and Atmospheric Administration (NOAA) satellite at 5:44 a.m. and 9:51 a.m. (Beijing time) on August 2, 2010. The first image showed a polluted area of sea near Shanhaiguan * Industry Co., Ltd. (the defendant), affecting about 5 square kilometers (km^2). The later image showed an abnormal area of polluted seawater about 4 kilometers (km) south of the defendant's enterprise, covering approximately 10 km^2.

Analyzing the pollution source, the IMFS ruled out the possibility of accidents such as red tides and large-scale oil spills, and concluded that the seawater pollution shown on the satellite image was caused by the discharge or leakage of sewage from a large enterprise. The defendant operated the only big factory close to the sea near Laolongtou, Shanhaiguan District, and its shipbuilding and repairing operations would produce a large amount of sewage. The high iron concentration in the sewage produced in the dock rust removal process would cause severe pollution to the nearby sea area, once that sewage had leaked. Given these indicators, the IMFS determined that the pollution was caused by the defendant, and the sewage leaked between approximately 12 midnight and 4 a.m. (Beijing time) on August 2, 2010.

Analyzing the pollution's impact on aquaculture, the IMFS confirmed the geographic coordinates of aquacultural areas run by 21 people (including Wang [surname]). By comparing these coordinates with the polluted waters on an electronic nautical chart, the forensic scientists concluded that all aquacultural areas were within the contaminated waters. Evaluating the water quality and environment, the IMFS concluded that the seawater contained high concentrations of suspended solids, iron, and petroleum hydrocarbons, which far exceeded the national standards specified in the Water Quality Standard for Fisheries and the Sea Water Quality Standard. The primary pollutant was iron, which presented a serious hazard to fisheries and aquaculture water. It was determined that the plaintiffs and others had suffered aquaculture losses.

The defendant submitted an opinion challenging the evidence of aquaculture losses found by the IMFS, mainly contending there was no factual or forensic basis for concluding that the seawater was polluted with an iron concentration higher than the limit. The defendant argued that the only data available to the IMFS in their evaluation of the water quality and environment of the aquacultural areas came from the EEB analysis, which did not meet the format and content requirements specified in the Specification for Marine Monitoring. The defendant also submitted that the standards adopted by the EEB in analyzing the iron concentration were for surface water, groundwater, and industrial wastewater, so their report lacked any probative value.

The defendant further contended that in the Water Quality Standard for Fisheries and Sea Water Quality Standard adopted by the IMFS, there was no provision or restriction on the iron concentration level in seawater, so this was not an indicator of water quality standards for marine fisheries, and even if iron concentration level were one of the indicators, there was no relevant standard regarding the quantity limit that constitutes pollution or damage.

During the trial, the IMFS submitted a further report clarifying their forensic methods of analysis, interpretations, and conclusions. The court-appointed scientists explained that since the gray value of the abnormal area of polluted seawater shown on the satellite images was slightly lower than that of the surrounding seawater, the possibility of red tides was excluded, and as there was no oil platform in the Laolongtou waters of Shanhaiguan, nor any large ship collision or grounding accident around 2 August, the possibility of oil spills was ruled out. Given these factors, the IMFS calculated that this pollution resulted from the discharge or leak of sewage by the only large enterprise likely to be producing substantial volumes of sewage close to the affected area, which was operated by the defendant.

Lv * Kui and 78 other persons filed a lawsuit for damages, claiming the red sewage discharged by the defendant had killed a large number of scallops, causing the plaintiffs to suffer heavy financial losses.

Judgments

On December 9, 2013, the Tianjin Maritime Court issued the [2011, Tianjin, Maritime Court First Trial, No. 115] Civil Judgment, dismissing the claims of all 79 plaintiffs. Lv * Kui and 78 other individuals appealed. On December 11, 2014, the Tianjin High People's Court issued the Final Fourth Civil Judgment No. 22 (2014).

Reversing the lower court's decision, the appellate court ordered the defendant to compensate Wang * and 20 other plaintiffs for aquaculture losses worth a total of CNY1,377,696 within 15 days from the date on which judgment was served. It dismissed the other claims of Lv * Kui and 78 other persons.

Reasoning

The court held that according to Article 66 of the Tort Law of the People's Republic of China, where any dispute arises over environmental pollution, the polluter shall assume the burden to prove that it should not be liable, or that its liability could be mitigated under certain circumstances provided for by law, or that there is no causation between its conduct and the harmful consequences.

It was held that Lv * Kui and 78 other persons must prove that the defendant's conduct caused pollution, and that this conduct caused damage to the plaintiffs' interests. It was also held that the plaintiffs must submit prima facie evidence of a causal relationship between the damage and the conduct causing pollution. To prove the pollution happened as a matter of fact, the plaintiffs submitted the IMFS and EEB reports as evidence.

Regarding the probative value of such evidence, the trial court had commissioned the IMFS to conduct a forensic appraisal, based on the plaintiffs' request. The remit of the IMFS covers maritime forensic appraisal, and each of their three forensic agents had the required qualifications, confirmed by the court. Moreover, the IMFS report, a statement made by the authority of Shanhaiguan District of Qinhuangdao in the Records of Inquiries, and a letter issued by the EEB corroborate each other. Such evidence proved that the Laolongtou sea area of Shanhaiguan was polluted on August 2, 2010.

Article 95(1) of the Marine Environmental Protection Law of the People's Republic of China defines "pollution damage to the marine environment" as "any direct or indirect introduction of substances or energy into the marine environment that results in deleterious effects, such as harm to marine living resources, hazards to human health, a hindrance to fishing and other legitimate activities at sea, impairment of the useful quality of seawater, and degradation of environmental quality." The IMFS report confirmed the gray value of the abnormal area of polluted seawater was slightly lower than that of the surrounding seawater, excluding the possibility of red tides. Since there was no oil platform in the Laolongtou waters and no large ship collision or grounding accident occurring around August 2, 2010, the possibility of oil spills was also ruled out.

The EEB report showed the seawater was reddish-brown and turbid, with an iron concentration of 13.1 mg/L, so it was concluded that the pollution was caused by dire discharge or leakage of sewage.

Moreover, as the defendant operated the only large enterprise close to the sea near Laolongtou, its main business was shipbuilding and repairing, and it was concluded that the pollution was caused by the defendant's leak of sewage containing high iron concentration levels from the rust removal process during the building and repairing of large ships.

Although not agreeing with the conclusion of the IMFS, the defendant failed to provide sufficient evidence and reasons to refute it—so the probative value of the pollution source analysis in the IMFS report was confirmed.

On whether the interests of Lv * Kui and 78 other persons were harmed: after analyzing the polluted sea area by confirming geographic coordinates of the aquacultural areas run by 21 people, including Wang (surname), then comparing these coordinates with those of the polluted waters on an electronic nautical chart, the IMFS concluded that all their aquacultural areas had been polluted.

On the causal relationship between conduct that caused pollution and the damage: while satisfying the burden of proof that the defendant's conduct caused pollution, and that such conduct damaged their interests, Wang and the 20 other plaintiffs were required to submit prima facie evidence proving a causal relationship between the damage and the conduct causing pollution.

According to the EEB sampling tests, water in that area had high concentration levels of suspended solids, iron, and petroleum hydrocarbons; but the primary pollutant was iron, presenting a serious hazard to fisheries and the aquaculture water. Therefore, Wang and the 20 other plaintiffs discharged their burden of proof.

Since the defendant claimed it was not the tortfeasor, it was required to prove that it should not be liable, that its liability could be mitigated under certain lawful circumstances, or that there was no causation between its conduct and the harm. The defendant claimed the standards adopted in the IMFS report had no provision or restriction on the iron concentration levels in seawater, so this was not an indicator of water quality standards. The defendant argued that even if iron concentration level were one of the indicators, there was no relevant standard regarding the quantity that constitutes pollution or damage.

On this issue, the court held that: Firstly, the Marine Environmental Protection Law of the People's Republic of China clearly provides that the introduction of substances or energy into the marine environment which results in deleterious effects is deemed pollution. In Article 65 of the Tort Law of the People's Republic of China, the liability for environmental pollution is not limited to the discharge of pollutants exceeding limits set in national or local standards. Therefore, regardless of whether discharge control requirements for certain substances are stipulated in the national or local standards, or whether the pollutant discharge meets the national or local standards, the polluter shall be liable for damages as long as its pollution conduct has caused environmental damage. Secondly, the Water Quality Standard for Fisheries and Sea Water Quality Standard (Standards) currently used for the evaluation of seawater quality in the People's Republic of China (PRC) have not been revised for a long time since their implementation, so those Standards may not cover all substances that can cause pollution in modern times. Therefore, the Standards are not the only basis for judging whether certain substances cause pollution damage.

Thirdly, the EEB also stated that pollutant discharge standards for iron concentration in seawater are not clearly stipulated in the PRC's regulations or codes, so this requires further discussion by experts from relevant authorities to determine whether iron concentration in water impacts aquaculture.

In this case, the IMFS scientists had the requisite expertise to identify marine pollution, and had concluded that the levels of iron in the affected seawater were hazardous to fisheries and aquaculture. Accepting this forensic evidence, the courts found that the water had indeed been polluted by iron.

Courts and Members of the Collegial Bench

Court of First Instance: In Tianjin Maritime Court, before Wang Zhunian, Pei Daming, Bian Hong

Court of Second Instance: In Tianjin High People's Court, before Geng Xiaoning, Tang Na, Li Shanchuan

Chapter 25
Li * vs. * Property (Chongqing) Co., Ltd. Over Liability for Light Pollution

Keywords Civil · Liability for environmental pollution · Light pollution · Damage determination · Tolerance level

Key Points

Due to the potential, invisible and individually varying harm of light pollution to people, the court shall determine the damage caused by light pollution in a comprehensive way based on: (i) national, local, and industry standards; (ii) whether it has a negative impact upon the normal lives, work, and study of others; and (iii) whether it exceeds public tolerance, etc.

Public tolerance can be ascertained from the reactions of surrounding residents, the actual experience in specific locations, and expert opinions, etc.

Basic Facts

The plaintiff, Li *, purchased an apartment on Xiejiawan Main Street in the Jiulongpo District of Chongqing, and has been living in it since 2005. The MixC, a shopping mall developed by the defendant, * Property (Chongqing) Co., Ltd., is separated from the plaintiff's residence by a two-way six-lane road, with a light rail line in the middle of this road. There are no other obstructions between the MixC and the plaintiff's residence. An LED advertising screen (screen) on the exterior wall of the MixC, facing the plaintiff's residence, has been in operation since its installation in 2014, displaying promotional materials and video commercials every day, generating strong light directly into the plaintiff's residence, which has affected his life.

Influential Environment and Resources Cases in China (2024),
https://doi.org/10.1007/978-981-96-9562-1_25

In May 2014, property owners in the plaintiff's apartment complex lodged a complaint with the municipal government, alleging that since 3 May, the giant screen had been generating strong light that cast into their rooms, causing serious light pollution, which affected their day-to-day lives. The property owners requested that the relevant authority order the screen's operators to reduce its volume and brightness.

In September 2014, property owners in * Complex, Huangyang Road, also lodged a complaint with the municipal government, alleging the screen kept displaying promotional information and commercials all night and every day, producing light that was too dazzling for people to sleep and rest at night normally. Claiming light pollution from the screen at night seriously affected nearby residents, property owners in * Complex, Huangyang Road requested that relevant authorities address this issue by forbidding screen displays at night, or by only allowing the display until 8 p.m., and by dimming its brightness.

In February 2018, property owners in the plaintiff's apartment complex lodged a further complaint with the municipal government, alleging the screen was a "nightmare" for nearby residents as it displayed video commercials every day, and the light was extremely strong and flashed frequently, so residents suffered from strong light exposure—akin to daytime—even at night, which seriously deprived the elderly and children of sleep. It was requested that the relevant authorities address this issue as soon as possible.

During the trial, on August 11, 2018, the court summoned the parties to an evening site inspection. The screen facing the plaintiff's apartment was playing video commercials and the strong light generated was cast into the plaintiff's residence. That night, the screen displayed video commercials until 8:58 p.m. According to the defendant, the size of the screen was 160 square meters (m^2).

On the issue of whether environmental monitoring can be conducted on such light pollution, the court consulted with the Ecology and Environment Monitoring Station (EMS) in Jiulongpo District, Chongqing.

According to the director of the EMS, they could not undertake environmental monitoring of the light pollution as there were no norms or technical indicators in place at the state or municipal level for the monitoring of such pollution.

According to the deputy head of the EMS in Yongchuan District, Chongqing, a member of the expert panel of the Chongqing court for trials on environmental resources, there was no specific standard for light pollution in terms of environmental protection, but it was possible to determine whether light pollution is caused based on the comprehensive assessment of the remaining evidence from the perspective of civil legal relations.

Based on evidence submitted by the plaintiff, damage caused by the screen was an objective reality, namely disturbance to the plaintiff's rest and sleep.

On the issue of light radiation generated by the screen, the court consulted a professor from the School of Architecture and Urban Planning of Chongqing University, the Vice President of the China Illuminating Engineering Society, a senior engineer from the School of Architecture and Urban Planning of Chongqing University, a director of the China Illuminating Engineering Society, and other experts.

According to these experts, light radiation from an LED screen has effects on human eyesight including disability glare and discomfort glare. This light radiation also has biological effects.

People gradually fall asleep as light intensity decreases at night, due to the effects of two hormones: melatonin and cortisol. Melatonin levels rise at night and fall during the day, while cortisol levels change conversely. Overly strong light radiation disrupts human biological clocks, and has long-term effects. In addition, blue light emitted by an LED screen causes damage to people's retinas, and can lead to irreparable loss of vision.

However, it was difficult to monitor the hazard presented by outdoor blue light, with no currently available standards to determine the effects of duration and intensity. Although some studies concluded that the impact of brightness on humans is lower if below 400 candela per square meter (cd/m^2), this standard was difficult to apply to dynamic advertising screens. For brightness standards, the specifications compiled by authorities in different sectors have different limits on brightness, but as LED screens were different from direct light generated for practical purposes, it was more appropriate to determine the impact of brightness on people in this case based on the national standards for LED displays.

Judgment

On December 28, 2018, the People's Court of Jiangjin District of Chongqing issued the [2018, Chongqing, 0116, Civil First Trial, No.6093] Civil Judgment.

As part of its order that the defendant immediately stop causing light pollution to the plaintiff by the screen's operation, the court directed that: (i) from 1 May to 30 September, the screen could only display after 8:30 a.m. and must cease before 10 p.m.; (ii) from 1 October to 30 April, the screen could only start after 8:30 a.m. and must cease before 9:30 p.m.; and (iii) after 7 p.m., the screen's brightness must not be higher than 600 cd/m^2. The plaintiff's remaining claims were rejected. Neither party appealed, nor the judgment was executed.

Reasoning

The court held that environmental protection is a basic national policy of the PRC, and all organizations and individuals are obliged to protect the environment. According to Article 9 of the General Provisions of the Civil Code of the People's Republic of China, "When conducting a civil activity, a person of the civil law shall act in a manner that facilitates conservation of resources and protection of the ecological environment."

According to Article 90 of the Property Law of the People's Republic of China, "A holder of real property may not discard solid wastes or discharge atmospheric pollutants, water pollutants, or such harmful substances as noise, light and magnetic radiation by violating the relevant provisions of the state."

According to Article 42(1) of the Environmental Protection Law of the People's Republic of China, "Businesses, non-profit institutions and other producers and business operators that discharge pollutants shall take measures to prevent and control the environmental pollution caused by waste gas, wastewater, waste residues, dust, malodorous gases, radioactive substances and noise, vibration, light radiation and electromagnetic radiation generated during production, construction or other activities."

This case involved disputed liability for environmental protection. According to Article 65 of the Tort Law of the People's Republic of China, "Where any harm is caused by environmental pollution, the polluter shall assume the tort liability." Environmental pollution tort liability is a special tort liability, and its constituent elements include three aspects: (i) the polluter's conduct caused environmental pollution; (ii) the plaintiff can prove the fact of harm; and (iii) there is a causal relationship between the polluter's conduct of polluting the environment and harm to the plaintiff's interests.

1. On whether the defendant engaged in conduct that polluted the environment:

As developer and operator of the MixC shopping mall, the defendant installed an LED screen on its exterior wall facing the plaintiff's residence, to display promotional content, and the strong light generated was cast directly into the plaintiff's home. According to the evidence, including the plaintiff's photos and videos, as well as information collected after both parties attended the court's site inspection, it could be determined that strong light generated by the defendant's screen exceeded the general public tolerance range: such bright light seriously affected the normal work and study of surrounding residents, disrupting their normal lives and rest, and constituted light pollution. The defendant's use of the screen for displaying commercials and promotional information caused light pollution, which constituted an act of polluting the environment.

2. On facts of harm to the plaintiff's interests:

Harm caused by environmental pollution mainly includes damage to the property and health of the plaintiff and the environment. Consequential damages from the tort of environmental pollution are different from the consequential damages of general torts, including not only damage with obvious and measurable symptoms, but also damage that is not obvious, or is temporarily asymptomatic, and cannot always be measured. Harm caused to humans by light pollution may be latent and invisible. Typically, the plaintiff does not have obvious symptoms of damage at the beginning of the victimization process, and the damage suffered often cannot be measured accurately; but such harm will manifest itself as time elapses. As described by experts in this case, light pollution has a perceptible impact on human vision, and overly strong light radiation disrupts a person's circadian clock, with long-term consequences instead of any discernible short-term impact.

In this case, strong light from the defendant's screen exceeded levels that ordinary people could tolerate, affecting the normal lives and rest of the plaintiff and surrounding residents. According to common sense, such light pollution was bound to damage the plaintiff's physical and mental health, environmental rights and interests.

3. On whether the defendant should bear tortious liability for environmental pollution:

According to Article 66 of the Tort Law of the People's Republic of China, "Where any dispute arises over an environmental pollution, the polluter shall assume the burden to prove that it should not be liable or its liability could be mitigated under certain circumstances as provided for by law or to prove that there is no causation between its conduct and the harm."

In this case, the plaintiff provided evidence to prove the defendant's conduct of polluting the environment, and the fact of damage caused to the plaintiff. The defendant assumed the burden to prove that either it should not be liable, or its liability could be mitigated under certain circumstances as provided for by law, or that there was no causation between its conduct of polluting the environment and the harm. However, the defendant did not submit evidence to discharge this burden of proof, so it would have to bear tortious liability for polluting the environment. According to Article 13 of the Interpretation of the Supreme People's Court of Several Issues on the Application of Law in the Trial of Disputes over Liability for Environmental Torts, "The people's court shall, based on the infringed party's claims and specifics of the case, reasonably determine that the polluter bears civil liabilities for the pollution, such as stopping the infringing conduct, removing obstacles, eliminating danger, restoring the original state, making an apology, and compensating for losses." The damage of environmental tort is different from general damage to person and property, and there are unique requirements for the tort liability assumed by the polluter. Environmental tort is an infringement of the personal and property rights and interests of an unspecified majority of people in a certain area through the environment, and once there is damage that can be measured in a quantitative method; the consequences are often irreparable and cannot be eliminated. Therefore, in an environmental tort, the polluter committing an act of polluting the environment should bear the corresponding tort liability, even if there was no measurable damage as yet.

In this case, judging from the citizens' complaints, the defendant should have realized that the strong light emitted by its screen would affect the plaintiff and other nearby residents; then the defendant should have realized its obligation to take necessary measures that reduced the impact on them.

However, the defendant continued to use the screen, and its bright light exceeded the level that ordinary people could tolerate, causing light pollution and seriously affecting the normal lives of the plaintiff and other residents, which caused harm to environmental rights and interests, as well as the physical and mental health of the plaintiffs and others involved. Therefore, even if the plaintiff had no obvious symptoms, it was a fact that the plaintiff's life was disrupted by light pollution and his environmental rights and interests had been damaged, so the defendant was liable for the tort, and under a duty to remove the nuisance.

Court and Members of the Collegial Bench

Court of First Instance: In Jiangjin Primary People's Court, Chongqing, beofore Jiang Ling, Luo Jing, Zhang Zhigui

Chapter 26
Civil Public Interest Litigation of China * Environmental Protection Foundation vs. * Glass Qinhuangdao Co., Ltd. Over Liability for Air Pollution

Keywords Civil · Environmental civil public interest litigation · Liability for air pollution · Environmental risk reduction · Mitigation of compensation liability

Key Points

In environmental civil public interest litigation, the court may consider a polluter taking the initiative to improve environmental protection facilities and effectively reducing environmental risks in mitigation of the polluter's liability, in addition to considerations about the degree of fault in discharging any unlawful pollutant and the costs of controlling such pollution.

Basic Facts

The defendant, * Glass Qinhuangdao Co., Ltd., was mainly engaged in the production and processing of glass bottles for packaging, using four glass furnaces. The Environmental Protection Bureau (EPB) of Haigang District, Qinhuangdao, repeatedly imposed administrative penalties on the defendant for the excessive discharge of pollutants during its operations.

On February 12, 2015, the defendant signed a contract with Wuxi * Environmental Protection Co., Ltd., worth CNY36.17 million, for denitration, desulfurization, and dust removal in the defendant's four glass furnaces.

In 2016, the China * Environmental Protection Foundation (plaintiff) brought an environmental public interest lawsuit against the defendant. After this suit was filed,

Influential Environment and Resources Cases in China (2024),
https://doi.org/10.1007/978-981-96-9562-1_26

the defendant accelerated its transformation toward denitrification, desulfurization, and dust removal.

On June 15, 2016, the defendant passed an environmental protection test organized by the EPB. On July 22, 2016, the plaintiff organized experts to inspect operations of the defendant's equipment for denitrification, desulfurization and dust removal, and made suggestions.

On June 17, 2016, and June 17, 2017, the EPB granted the defendant Pollutant Discharge Permits in Hebei Province. On December 2, 2016, the defendant invested a further CNY19.65 million to add auxiliary equipment for denitration, desulfurization, and dust removal in its four furnaces.

The defendant paid an administrative fine of CNY80,000 on March 18, 2015. After the plaintiff filed suit in 2016, the defendant paid further administrative fines of CNY12.81 million in 24 installments, from April 13 to November 23, 2016.

On July 25, 2017, the plaintiff submitted "Notes on Claims and Evidence" to the court, contending that the period of environmental harm caused by the defendant's illegal discharge of air pollutants should run from the date it was noted by an administrative agency to the date when the defendant passed the EPB's environmental protection acceptance test.

The court commissioned the Center for Environmental Damage and Risk Assessment (CEDRA), under the Chinese Academy of Environmental Planning, to appraise the environmental damage caused by the defendant's emission of air pollutants and to assess the cost of ecological restoration measures for the polluted atmosphere, from October 28, 2015 (when harm was noted by the administrative agency) to June 15, 2016 (when the defendant passed the EPB test).

In November 2017, CEDRA reported its findings. Based on the virtual cost approach, the total amount of particulates discharged into the air by the defendant during the appraisal period was about 2.06 tons; sulfur dioxide exceeded the standard limit by about 33.45 tons; and nitrogen oxides exceeded the standard limit by about 75.33 tons. As the air zone in the defendant's area was classified as "Class II," regulations deemed the monetary amount of ecological damage to be 3~5 times the virtual governance costs. Calculated by three times the amount in CEDRA's report, the damage caused by discharging these identified pollutants into the atmosphere in monetary terms was about CNY7,400, CNY271,000, and CNY1,271,200, respectively—totaling CNY1,549,600.

Reports were also noted on the websites of Hebei Broadcasting Network and Hebei News in March 2015 which revealed that the defendant was fined more than CNY2 million for discharging air pollutants exceeding the standard limits over several days, and for failing to install dust removal, denitrification, and desulfurization facilities. Accepting the accuracy of those online news reports, the defendant acknowledged it had discharged pollutants exceeding the standard limits before October 28, 2015.

Judgment

On April 10, 2018, the Qinhuangdao Intermediate People's Court, Hebei Province, delivered the[2016, Hebei, 03, Civil First Trial, No.40] Civil Judgment:

1. The defendant was ordered to pay CNY1,549,600 in damages for the loss caused by the excessive discharge of air pollutants, into the special fund account of Qinhuangdao Municipality, for environmental restoration in Qinhuangdao. This was to be paid in three installments of CNY516,500: the first within 7 days of the judgment's execution and the second and third installments before 31 December of the second and third year respectively after the judgment's execution.
2. Within 30 days of the judgment's execution, the defendant was required to make an apology in national media for polluting the atmosphere—this statement was to be reviewed by the court of first instance, before publication. The order noted that if the defendant failed to fulfill these obligations, the Qinhuangdao Intermediate People's Court would release the content of this judgment in national media, with the relevant expenses to be borne by the defendant.
3. The defendant was ordered to pay the plaintiff CNY30,000 for reasonable expenses incurred in this case, within 15 days after this judgment's execution.
4. The plaintiff's other claims were rejected. The defendant was ordered to pay the court fee of CNY80, plus the plaintiff's appraisal, and assessment costs of CNY150,000.

The plaintiff appealed. On November 5, 2018, the Hebei High People's Court issued the (2018) [Hebei Civil Final] No. 758 Civil Judgment, dismissing the appeal and affirming the trial court's judgment.

Reasoning

The court held that, according to Article 23 of the Interpretation of the Supreme People's Court on Several Issues concerning the Application of Law in the Trial of Environmental Civil Public Interest Litigation Cases: "If it is difficult to determine the cost of ecological restoration, the people's court may reasonably determine the restoration cost by considering the scope and degree of environmental pollution and ecological damage and factors such as the cost of operating pollution prevention facilities, the benefits obtained by the polluter from the tort, and the degree of fault." In February 2015, to upgrade environmental protection facilities in its four glass furnaces, the defendant signed a CNY36.17 million contract with Wuxi * Environmental Protection Co., Ltd. for denitration, desulfurization, and dust removal. This reflected the defendant's law-abiding awareness of pollution prevention and rectification issues.

However, the defendant discharged excessive pollutants during the upgrading and transformation of its environmental protection facilities. Although its conduct was unlawful, the defendant paid fines of more than CNY12.8 million in administrative penalties for its excessive discharge of pollutants. After this public interest lawsuit was filed, the defendant accelerated its upgrading of environmental protection facilities by investing a further CNY19.65 million in auxiliary equipment regulating pollutant discharge, to pass the environmental protection acceptance test—becoming the first enterprise in Qinhuangdao to keep two sets of environmental protection equipment in operation, with one set redundant, as part of its air pollution control efforts.

In Articles 1 and 4 of the Environmental Protection Law of the People's Republic of China, it is clearly stated that the legislative intent is to protect the environment, prevent pollution, and promote sustainable economic development, reflecting the principle of putting equal emphasis on environmental protection and economic growth.

While emphasizing the importance of environmental damage relief, environmental public interest litigation should also attach importance to preemptive measures.

During this litigation, the defendant accelerated the rectification of its environmental protection capacity, discharged administrative liabilities, and invested nearly CNY20 million in facilities after installed equipment passed the acceptance test, to ensure stable production operations—significantly reducing the risk of causing further environmental pollution.

The defendant voluntarily invested a substantial sum in pollution prevention and control, serving the public interest and surpassing the claim of "compensating environmental damage and environmental restoration" made by the plaintiff at trial. Such action also satisfied Article 5 of the Environmental Protection Law of the People's Republic of China, which requires "protection and prevention first," as well as the risk prevention purposes and guiding principles of environmental civil public interest litigation.

The court took all factors into consideration, including the illegality of the defendant's excessive discharge of pollutants in the production process, the degree of fault, and the operating cost of pollution control facilities—as well as the measures taken by the defendant for pollution prevention and control, mitigating the damage caused. Accordingly, the appeal court upheld the trial court's judgment based on the appraisal report, without modifying the damages awarded for environmental damage and restoration costs.

Court and Members of the Collegial Bench

Court of First Instance: In Qinhuangdao Intermediate People's Court, Hebei, before Liu Ziming, Dai Zhenxi, Chen Caidong

Court of Second Instance: In Hebei High People's Court, before Dou Shuxia, Li Xuejing, Xing huili

Chapter 27
Jiangsu Provincial People's Government vs. Anhui * Chemical Co., Ltd. Over Ecological and Environmental Damage Compensation

Keywords Civil · Ecological damage compensation litigation · Installment payment

Key Points

Enterprises, Non-profit public institutions, producers, and business operators transferring their hazardous wastes to organizations or individuals unqualified for its disposal, shall be liable for environmental damage caused by pollution. The court may consider factors including the subjective faults and business conditions of such waste-generating entities, and may order defendants to pay damages in installments, after providing security.

Basic Facts

On April 28, 2014, the defendant's marketing manager, Yang *, transferred 29.1 tons of the company's waste lye from the defendant's production process to Sheng *, an individual who had no qualifications for hazardous waste disposal. Sheng and others transferred the waste lye to Sun *, who also had no qualifications for hazardous waste disposal. On April 30, 2014, Sun * and others dumped the waste lye into the Yangtze River, causing major environmental pollution. On May 7, 2014, Yang * transferred a further 20 tons of the defendant's waste lye to Sheng * and others for disposal, who then passed it again to Sun * for disposal. On May 7 and June 17, 2014, Sun * and others dumped waste lye into the Yangtze River, interrupting the centralized drinking water supply in Jingjiang, Jiangsu Province for over 40 hours from 9 to 11 May.

Influential Environment and Resources Cases in China (2024),
https://doi.org/10.1007/978-981-96-9562-1_27

From 8 to 9 May 2014, Yang * transferred a further 53.34 tons of waste lye to Sheng * and others for disposal; Sheng * and others passed this to Ding * for disposal. Ding * and others dumped the waste lye into the New Tongyang Canal on May 14, 2014, which interrupted water intake for the centralized drinking water supply in Xinghua, Jiangsu Province, for more than 14 hours.

After the pollution occurred, the Jingjiang Municipal Environmental Protection Bureau and the Jingjiang Municipal People's Procuratorate jointly commissioned the Jiangsu Society for Environmental Sciences (JSES) to conduct an assessment of pollution damage. Following investigations and evaluations, JSES reported its findings in June 2015. The Jiangsu Provincial People's Government filed a lawsuit in the Taizhou Intermediate People's Court of Jiangsu Province, requesting that the defendant be ordered to pay CNY36,379,000 in damages for ecological restoration costs; CNY18,189,500 for the loss of ecological service functions; and CNY260,000 for evaluation and litigation costs.

Judgments

On August 16, 2018, the Taizhou Intermediate People's Court of Jiangsu Province delivered the [2017, Jiangsu, 12, Civil First Trial, No.51] Civil Judgment:

1.1. The defendant, Anhui * Chemical Co., Ltd., shall pay (i) CNY36,379,000 in damages for environmental restoration costs; (ii) CNY18,189,500 for the loss of ecological service functions; and (iii) CNY260,000 for the evaluation costs.

The defendant appealed, and the Jiangsu High People's Court issued the (2018) [Jiangsu, Civil, Final] No. 1316 Civil Judgment on December 4, 2018:

1. Affirming the trial court's judgment, the appellant was ordered to pay compensation of CNY54,828,500 into the bank account for Taizhou environmental public interest litigations within 60 days from the date of this judgment's execution.
2. The appellant was ordered to pay 20% (CNY10,965,700) of the total amount within 60 days of this judgment's execution, after providing effective security to the trial court; annual installments of 20% of the total (CNY10,965,700) were to be paid on 4 December of each successive year until 2022. If any installment was not made on time, the Jiangsu Provincial People's Government could apply to the court for mandatory enforcement of all unpaid damages. If the appellant failed to perform its payment obligations on time, it would be required to pay double the amount of the debt interest during the delayed performance period, in accordance with Article 253 of the Civil Procedure Law of the People's Republic of China.

Reasoning

The court held that the defendant, as a chemical enterprise, had the obligation to prevent environmental pollution from the hazardous waste lye generated during its production and business operation. The defendant allowed Yang *, head of its marketing department, to transfer the waste lye to individuals who were not qualified for hazardous waste disposal, resulting in the waste being dumped into the Yangtze River and the New Tongyang Canal, substantially polluting the environment.

According to Article 64 of the Environmental Protection Law of the People's Republic of China, those who cause damages due to environmental pollution and ecological destruction shall bear tort liability in accordance with Article 65 of the Tort Law of the People's Republic of China: where any harm is caused by environmental pollution, the polluter shall assume the tort liability.

Further, according to Article 15, the methods of assuming tort liabilities shall include restoration of the environment to its original status, and compensation for losses. Compensation for environmental restoration costs, loss of ecological service functions, and assessment fees are all specific means of assuming such tort liabilities.

In accordance with Article 15(1), item 6, and Article 65 of the Tort Law of the People's Republic of China, as well as Article 1(1) and Article 13 of the Interpretation of the Supreme People's Court of Several Issues on the Application of Law in the Trial of Disputes over Liability for Environmental Torts, it was appropriate to order the defendant to pay damages for its tort liability.

The defendant applied for leave to pay compensation in installments on the grounds it was experiencing financial hardship and would face bankruptcy if all the damages had to be paid by lump sum.

To strike an effective balance between ecological protection and economic growth, the Jiangsu Provincial People's Government stated, after the hearing that if the defendant could provide evidence to prove its business was aligned with the direction of national economic restructuring and could transition to green production, the defendant would be allowed to pay damages in five installments, in accordance with Article 231 of the Civil Procedure Law of the People's Republic of China—on the condition that the defendant could provide effective security.

Courts and Members of the Collegial Bench

Court of First Instance: In Taizhou Intermediate People's Court, Jiangsu, before Gu Jincai, Cao Haixia, Su Yuanyuan

Court of Second Instance: In Jiangsu High People's Court, before Chen Ying, Zhao Li, Wu Xiaoling

Chapter 28
Environmental Administrative Public Interest Litigation of Jianchuan County People's Procuratorate of Yunnan Province vs. Forest Public Security Bureau of * County for Neglect of Statutory Duties

Keywords Administrative · Environmental administrative public interest litigation · Neglect of statutory duties · Investigation standard

> **Key Points**
> In environmental administrative public interest litigation, the court shall determine whether an administrative agency has discharged its statutory duties by examining: (i) whether the perpetrator's illegal acts have been effectively suspended; (ii) whether the agency has adopted statutory regulatory measures adequately, timely, and effectively; and (iii) whether the national or public interests have been effectively protected.

Basic Facts

In January 2013, Wang * Quan(Wang*), a resident of Jianchuan County, was commissioned by Yuxin Company (Yuxin) to excavate for a road in a state-owned forest zone. His action was discovered and stopped by forest rangers of the Hongqi Forestry Bureau of Jianchuan County, which then passed the case to the Forest Public Security Bureau of * County (defendant) for investigation.

On February 20, 2013, the defendant served Wang * with notice of the right to a hearing on forestry administrative punishment. On February 27, 2013, the defendant delivered to Wang * its No. 288 Written Decision on the Forestry Administrative Penalty [Jianchuan Forestry Penalty] (2013) (FAP), which stated: "Without obtaining any legal forest land acquisition and occupation permit, Yuxin Company commissioned Wang * to use an excavator to excavate for a road with a length of 494.8 m

Influential Environment and Resources Cases in China (2024),
https://doi.org/10.1007/978-981-96-9562-1_28

and an average width of 4.5 m, covering an area of 2226.6 square meters, totaling 0.55 acres." In accordance with Article 43(1) of the Regulations on the Implementation of the Forest Law of the People's Republic of China, it was decided to impose administrative penalties on Wang * and Yuxin, requiring them to: (i) restore the land to its original status within a time limit; and (ii) pay CNY10 per square meter of illegally changed forest land, totaling CNY22,266.

After Yuxin paid the fine on March 29, 2013, the defendant closed the case. However, it failed to supervise and ensure that Yuxin and Wang * performed their obligation to restore the land and damaged forest vegetation to its original status within a time limit.

On November 9, 2016, the Jianchuan County People's Procuratorate (Procuratorate) issued Procuratorial Advice to the defendant, suggesting that it should perform its duties in accordance with the law, conscientiously implement the administrative penalty decision, and take effective measures to restore forest vegetation.

On December 8, 2016, the defendant replied that it had immediately conducted serious research after receiving the Procuratorial Advice and took proactive measures. It sent police to Wang's residence to remind him to implement the FAP and restore the land to its original status; but this implementation process had been terminated in view of Wang's death. The defendant did not issue any reminder notice to Yuxin.

The court also found that the defendant was a section-level institution under the Forestry Bureau of Jianchuan County (FBJC). In early 2013, the FBJC authorized the defendant to handle all forestry and forest land penalties in the county.

On September 27, 2013, the Yunnan Provincial People's Government (YPG) authorized all its forest public security departments to exercise forestry administrative punishment powers. On November 20, 2013, the YPG Legal Affairs Office announced the agencies qualified and authorized for forestry-related law enforcement, including the defendant.

On December 11, 2013, the Yunnan Provincial Forestry Department issued a notice approved by the YPG, stating that from January 1, 2014, all forest public security departments shall exercise 62 types of forestry administrative punitive power, and 11 types of administrative compulsory power.

Judgment

On August 19, 2017, the People's Court of Jianchuan County issued the [2017, Yunnan, 2931, Administrative First Trial, No.1] Administrative Judgment:

1. Confirming that the defendant's failure to perform the obligation specified in the FAP was unlawful; and
2. Ordering the defendant to discharge its statutory duties.

Neither party appealed. The judgment was executed, and the defendant performed its duties.

Reasoning

The court held that the public interest plaintiff filing a lawsuit was aligned with the scope of administrative public interest litigation stipulated in Implementing Measures for the Pilot Project for the Trial by People's Courts of Public Interest Litigation Cases Instituted by People's Procuratorate, issued by the Supreme People's Court, and Implementation Measures for the Pilot Project for the People's Procuratorate to Institute Public Interest Litigation, issued by the Supreme People's Procuratorate, and met the conditions for prosecution.

According to Article 26(6) of the Administrative Litigation Law of the People's Republic of China, "If an administrative agency has been abolished, the administrative agency that carries on the exercise of functions and powers of the abolished agency shall be the defendant."

On September 27, 2013, the YPG authorized all forest public security agencies to exercise some of the administrative punitive powers of the forestry administrative departments. Therefore, the defendant acquired forestry administrative punitive powers originally vested in the Forestry Bureau of Jianchuan County, making it the liable party.

In this case, after learning that Yuxin and Wang * had changed the forest land without authorization, the defendant—in the name of the Forestry Bureau of Jianchuan County—ordered Yuxin and Wang * to restore the land to its original status within a time limit and to pay a fine of CNY22,266. While that decision complied with the law, the defendant did not ensure Yuxin and Wang * restored the damaged forest land to its original status within three years after the fine was paid; nor did it perform the duty on their behalf.

Consequently, the forest land unlawfully altered by Yuxin and Wang * had not been restored to its original status, and no evidence was provided to prove any lawful excuses for this. The defendant's conduct was obviously improper, by failing to discharge its statutory duties: the administrative penalty decision had not been executed. The defendant had to perform its statutory duties according to the law, and take effective measures to ensure the altered forest land was restored to its original status within a reasonable time limit.

Court and Members of the Collegial Bench

Court of First Instance: In Jianchuan Primary People's Court, Yunnan, before Zhao Xinke, Bai Canshan, Zhang Jiyuan

Chapter 29
Chen * Long vs. Environmental Protection Bureau of * District, Chengdu Over Environmental Administrative Penalty

Keywords Administrative · Administrative penalty · Environmental protection · Installing concealed pipe without permit · Evasion of supervision

> **Key Points**
> Enterprises, non-profit institutions, producers, and business operators who discharge water pollutants by evading supervision by secretly installing concealed sewage pipes without a permit, shall be subject to administrative penalties according to the law. Where a polluter objects to administrative penalties by claiming the pollutants discharged meet standards and have caused no harm to the environment, the court will reject such a claim.

Basic Facts

The plaintiff Chen * Long was the owner of a glass factory in the Damian Community of Chengdu's Longquanyi District, processing and producing tempered glass since March 2011. On November 2, 2012, the Environmental Protection Bureau of * District (EPB) inspected the plaintiff's facilities and found the factory had a secret sewage pipe to discharge sewage without a permit. After investigation, the EPB issued an administrative penalty [* Environmental Punishment, 2012, No.1130-01] on December 11, 2012, stating the plaintiff's act violated Article 22(2) of the Law of the People's Republic of China on Prevention and Control of Water Pollution (CWP Law). In accordance with Article 75(2) of the CWP Law, a penalty decision was made, ordering the plaintiff to remove the concealed pipe immediately and pay a

Influential Environment and Resources Cases in China (2024),
https://doi.org/10.1007/978-981-96-9562-1_29

fine of CNY100,000. The plaintiff refused to accept the penalty and filed a lawsuit requesting the court to set it aside.

Judgment

On May 21, 2014, the People's Court of Chenghua District, Chengdu, Sichuan Province, dismissed the plaintiff's claims via the [2014, Chenghua, Administrative First Trial, No.29] Administrative Judgment. The plaintiff refused to comply and appealed to the Chengdu Intermediate People's Court, Sichuan Province.

On August 22, 2014, the Chengdu Intermediate People's Court dismissed the plaintiff's appeal via administrative judgment (Chengdu, Administrative, Final No. 345 Administrative Judgment).

On October 21, 2014, the plaintiff filed a motion with Chengdu Intermediate People's Court, seeking a retrial. In Chengdu, Administrative, No. 131, the court ruled against the plaintiff's motion.

Reasoning

The court held that while the plaintiff's factory was registered in Chengdu's Longquanyi District, it was in the city's * District where the violation of law occurred, resulting in environmental pollution during production and processing. According to Article 20 of the Law of the People's Republic of China on Administrative Penalty, and Article 17 of the Measures for Environmental Administrative Punishment, * EPB had the jurisdiction and administrative power to make the penalty decision.

A Test Report issued by the Environmental Monitoring Station of * District on May 22, 2012 showed that wastewater discharged by the plaintiff's factory met standards for discharging sewage; but as it was discharged through the concealed pipe installed without a permit, it violated Article 22(2) of the CWP Law.

Before this case, the plaintiff's factory had been subject to administrative penalties for the illegal act of "starting production without obtaining the environmental impact assessment permit and passing the environmental protection facilities acceptance test"—so this latest contravention constituted relapsing unlawful conduct. Therefore, within the penalty range specified in Article 75(2) of the CWP Law, and considering this case was the plaintiff's second breach of the law, it was appropriate for * EPB to impose the administrative penalty of CNY100,000.

Courts and Members of the Collegial Bench

Court of First Instance: In Chenghua Primary People's Court, Sichuan, before Xiang Zhengrong, Yin Hanchang, Gu Lihong

Court of Second Instance: In Chengdu Intermediate People's Court, Sichuan, before Li Weidong, Yu Xiaomin, Qiu Fangli

Chapter 30
Enforcement Supervision Case of Yu * Yan vs. * Mining LLC. in Xilin Gol League Over Transfer of Mining Rights

Keywords Enforcement · Supervision of enforcement · Transfer of mining rights · Assistance in enforcement · Administrative approval

Key Points

The court held that the parties' mining rights transfer contract was lawfully concluded, but had not yet been executed; the transferor was ordered to complete formalities for transferring mining rights in accordance with the contract—but this judgment was not concerned with determining ownership of the mining rights. Relying on the order, the enforcement court issued a notice to the competent authorities requesting assistance to complete the transfer of mining rights. But the notice was only used for requesting the competent authorities to initiate the review and approval process for the mining rights transfer; it should be decided by the competent authorities in accordance with the law whether the mining rights should be transferred.

Where the enforcement applicant sought to amen d the transferee of the mining rights, this should also be determined by the competent authorities in accordance with the law.

Basic Facts

On August 1, 2008, * Mining LLC. in Xilin Gol League (* Mining) signed a Mining Rights Transfer Contract (the contract) agreeing to transfer the mining rights for the Li Ying fluorite mine in the third production brigade of Bayantuga, Abaga Banner, to Yu * Yan (Yu *) for value. Yu * paid CNY1.5 million for this transfer of mining rights

Influential Environment and Resources Cases in China (2024),
https://doi.org/10.1007/978-981-96-9562-1_30

according to the contract, made a preliminary design for the mining area after taking possession, and began mining. However, * Mining failed to complete the mining rights transfer procedures for Yu * in accordance with the contract.

In October 2012, the parties' dispute was brought before the Intermediate People's Court of Xilin Gol League of Inner Mongolia Autonomous Region (XGL court). The XGL court held that the contract signed by * Mining and Yu * was based on the real intent of both parties, and the contract had been established in accordance with the law; but the contract could only take effect with the competent administrative agency's approval, according to laws and regulations. The transferee's eligibility to acquire mining rights was subject to the examination and approval of the administrative agency, not the court's jurisdiction.

Therefore, * Mining's claims that Yu * was not qualified to acquire mining rights as required by law, and that the court should invalidate their contract and order the payment of liquidated damages by Yu *, could not be upheld by the court.

Yu * counterclaimed for an order compelling * Mining to obtain the administrative approvals required for the transfer of the mining rights. Since the two parties clearly agreed in the contract that such approvals should be obtained by * Mining, the court upheld Yu*'s counterclaim.

However, Yu *'s claim that * Mining should pay liquidated damages was not upheld by the court because although the contract was legally concluded, it was pending approval and had not yet come into force—and liability for breach of contract was premised on the validity of the contract. The XGL court issued a civil judgment ordering * Mining, within 15 days of the judgment's execution, to complete the procedures required for their mining rights transfer approval in accordance with the contract.

Mining appealed. The High People's Court of the Inner Mongolia Autonomous Region (High Court of Inner Mongolia) held that the contract represented the parties' real intent, and was concluded with their signatures or seals. According to Article 44 of the Contract Law of the People's Republic of China, the contract concluded according to law becomes effective upon its execution. Where it is provided by laws or administrative regulations that formalities such as approval and registration shall be completed for a contract to take effect, such provisions shall be followed.

According to Article 10 of the Measures for the Administration of Transfer of Mineral Exploration Right and Mining Right, for applicants seeking the transfer of mineral exploration rights or mining rights, the examination and approval administration agency should—within 40 days from the date of receiving an application for transfer—decide whether to approve it and then inform the parties of its decision.

If the transfer is approved, the contract shall take effect on the day of approval.

If the transfer is not approved, the examination and approval administration agency should explain the reasons.

As stipulated in Article 9(1) of the Interpretation of the Supreme People's Court on Several Issues concerning the Application of the Contract Law of the People's Republic of China and in accordance with Article 44(2) of the Contract Law, where contracts are subject to approval or registration as provided by laws or administrative regulations, their provisions shall be followed.

If parties have not complied with registration or approval formalities before the end of the trial court's hearing, it shall determine the contract has not come into effect. The contract signed by both parties had not complied with the approval and registration formalities. Therefore, the contract was concluded according to law, but it had not come into force; its validity was to be determined.

Whether Yu * was qualified as a mining right transferee and whether the contract could be approved by the relevant authorities was not up to the court to decide. However, it was appropriate for the trial court to determine that the contract was lawfully concluded, and that * Mining should complete the transfer approval formalities for Yu * in accordance with the contract. If the administrative authority does not grant approval to the transfer proposed in the contract, both parties may claim their rights separately in accordance with the Contract Law. The High Court of Inner Mongolia issued a civil judgment affirming the original judgment.

Based on Yu *'s application, the XGL court filed a case for enforcement and issued an enforcement notice to * Mining, requiring it to perform the obligations prescribed by the effective judgment. Since * Mining did not perform the obligation, a notice of assistance in enforcement was issued to the Land and Resources Bureau of Xilin Gol League requesting the Bureau to assist Yu *, the applicant for enforcement, to complete the formalities required for administrative approval of the transfer according to the contract, in accordance with the effective judgment. The Bureau replied that after * Mining signed the contract with Yu *, * Mining did not submit a transfer application to the Bureau and that the contract was a mining rights transfer contract signed between a business and a natural person. According to the Bureau, as stipulated by laws, administrative regulations, and local regulations, the assistance in enforcement requested by the XGL court in the notice could not be provided.

On May 19, 2014, Yu * established the Xilin Gol League * Fluorite Sales Co., Ltd. (Fluorite Sales Company), solely owned by a natural person, and applied to the XGL court to assign the enforcement application to this company.

Judgment

On December 14, 2016, the XGL court issued an enforcement ruling [Xilin Gol, Intermediate, Execution, No.11], rejecting Yu *'s request to assign the enforcement application to Fluorite Sales Company.

Yu * appealed to the High People's Court of the Inner Mongolia Autonomous Region for reconsideration. On March 15, 2017, the High People's Court of the Inner Mongolia Autonomous Region issued an enforcement ruling [2017, Inner Mongolia, Execution, Reconsideration, No.4], dismissing Yu *'s application for reconsideration.

Yu * appealed to the Supreme People's Court. On December 26, 2017, the Supreme People's Court issued an enforcement ruling [2017, Supreme Court, Execution, No.136], dismissing Yu *'s appeal.

Reasoning

The Supreme People's Court held that the enforcement of this case was based on the agreement that * Mining should complete the mining rights transfer procedures for Yu * in accordance with the contract. According to current laws, in an application for the transfer of mineral exploration rights or mining rights, approval of the transfer should be obtained from the examination and approval administration agency before the transfer is made. If the transfer was approved, the contract should take effect on the day of approval. The courts of first and second instance held that the qualification of the transferee seeking mining rights was subject to the examination and approval of the administrative agency. Whether Yu * qualified as a mining rights transferee, and whether the contract could be approved by the relevant authorities, were not issues within the court's jurisdiction.

Since the contract had not yet been approved by the administrative agency, it was determined by the trial court that the contract was concluded according to law, but had not yet taken effect.

The appellate court also held that if the administrative agency did not approve the contract, the parties could assert their rights through other remedies regarding the legal consequences, rights, and obligations of the contract.

While the contract did not come into effect because the transfer had not been approved by the administrative authority, it did not compromise the validity of clauses in the contract requiring submission to the authority for approval; and combined with the reasons for judgment in this case, the order that "* Mining shall go through procedures required for the mining rights transfer approval in accordance with the Mining Rights Transfer Contract" was not a determination of the ownership of mining rights. The judgment referred to the fulfillment of an obligation to submit the contract for approval to render it effective, and the contract should be approved by the administrative agency before the registration of this transfer of mining rights. Therefore, the XGL court issued a notice to the Land and Resources Bureau of Xilin Gol League to assist in the transfer of mining rights, which was only equivalent to * Mining completing the application to the administrative authority for the transfer of mining rights and starting the examination and approval process by that administrative authority. This step could only be understood as requiring the Bureau to perform the function of examining and approving the transfer contract according to law.

Unlike general civil legal rights, mining rights required examination, approval, and licensing from administrative agencies. The rights of acceptance of an unapproved mining rights transfer contract were quite different from the rights of acceptance and transfer of creditor's rights in ordinary civil judgments.

The issue could not be resolved by applying to change the enforcement party in the enforcement procedure. In this case, Yu * claimed to satisfy approval formalities for the transfer of mining rights in the name of Flourite Sales Company, which he had established.

In essence, this issue still fell within the scope of administrative examination and approval, to determine whether the transferee of mining rights met the statutory requirements, and this should be decided by the administrative authority in accordance with regulations on the management of mining rights.

Believing he could fulfill rights and obligations determined by the legally effective judgment, Yu * established the Flourite Sales Company intending to meet the requirements for approval of the transfer in accordance with the administrative agency's provisions—which was not transferring the rights in the contract to a third party, nor did it harm the state's or any other party's interests.

Yu * also believed his application to satisfy transfer formalities under the Flourite Sales Company name complied with the: (i) Mineral Resources Law of the People's Republic of China; (ii) Interim Provisions on the Administration of the Assignment and Transfer of Mining Rights; (iii) Administrative Measures for the Registration of Mineral Resources Exploitation; (iv) Supplementary Notice on Regulating the Management of Prospecting Rights and Mining Rights, issued by the Department of Land and Resources of the Inner Mongolia Autonomous Region; and (v) other regulations on handling mining rights transfer procedures by administrative authority, in the case of a natural person signing a contract for the transfer of such rights. Therefore, this view should be asserted in a request to the administrative authority responsible for the examination and approval.

The XGL court and the High Court of Inner Mongolia rejected Yu *'s application for the transferee change, following opinions expressed in the binding judgment of this case on the approval of the contract—and the judgment did not conflict with the laws and judicial interpretations of the enforcement procedure.

Courts and Members of the Collegial Bench

Court of Enforcement: Xilingol Intermediate People's Court, Inner Mongolia, by Gao Long, Li Huilai, Qenggelehua Court of Enforcement Reconsideration: Inner Mongolia High People's Court, by Liang Jing, Yang Guofeng, Wang Guimei Court of Enforcement Supervision: Supreme People's Court of the People's Republic of China, by Huang Jinlong, Liu Shaoyang, Zhu Yan

MIX
Papier aus verantwortungsvollen Quellen
Paper from responsible sources
FSC® C105338
FSC
www.fsc.org

If you have any concerns about our products,
you can contact us on
ProductSafety@springernature.com

In case Publisher is established outside the EU,
the EU authorized representative is:
Springer Nature Customer Service Center GmbH
Europaplatz 3, 69115 Heidelberg, Germany

Printed by Libri Plureos GmbH
in Hamburg, Germany